THE HARD TWENTY SOMETHINGS

THE HARD TWENTY SOMETHINGS

O. Brent Dongell

TATE PUBLISHING
AND ENTERPRISES, LLC

Published by Tate Publishing & Enterprises, LLC
127 E. Trade Center Terrace | Mustang, Oklahoma 73064 USA
1.888.361.9473 | www.tatepublishing.com

Tate Publishing is committed to excellence in the publishing industry. The company reflects the philosophy established by the founders, based on Psalm 68:11,
"The Lord gave the word and great was the company of those who published it."

Book design copyright © 2013 by Tate Publishing, LLC. All rights reserved.
Cover design by Rtor Maghuyop
Interior design by Ronnel Luspoc

Published in the United States of America

ISBN: 978-1-62295-439-1
1. Religion / Christian Life / Spiritual Growth
2. Self-Help / Personal Growth / Happiness
13.05.01

THANK YOU

Thank you. I cannot say thank you enough to the most loving and insightful God and people all around me. This literally would be nonexistent without them.

Thank you Mom, Dad, Jen, Brandon, Kelly, and Brenton for being the Christian influences and examples that offer me so much strength and love, it's impossible to hoard and not share this love with others.

Thank you to all of my friends, family, and church community that are too numerous to count. To all of you who have shared in the excitement and processed through this season of life with me. Trace, Erika, Underground, Levi, Sara, Bekah, Becca, Taylor, Evy, John, Meg, Lindsey, Emma, Kevin, Katie, Christy, Paul, Brett, Carys, Mackays, and the list goes on.

Thank you, God, for this humbling opportunity. I am praying that You get the glory.

The Logic

I Fall Asleep Reading Books

Do you think books are too long? I did growing up. One of the most frustrating things about writing this book is that I would've fallen asleep reading it ten years ago. I was not a reader. I was the athlete that fell asleep sitting still. So how do I write a book, for that guy? Oh, you know: draw some pictures… laugh at myself… give shortcuts if you want them. If you are a mac daddy stud or studdette reader, read the whole thing and you won't regret it. If you are a mac daddy stud or studdette at something else and simply want a shorter option, check out the next two pages.

The Short God Book

The Short Picture Book

Prologue

The expectation hangover. Five years, one hundred documents, 500-1000 pages of content later, and I come up with a book that may not even be worth one hundred pages. It doesn't feel completely settled. But when I look at Jesus healing ten lepers and only one returning to say thanks, or Him leaving the ninety-nine to go after the one, or the Father of Nations taking one hundred years to produce two sons, or king David never getting to build the temple he wanted, or only two of the twelve spies getting to the enter the Promised Land, excluding Moses who led the people faithfully through the desert, I realize life's never going to turn out and feel exactly how I expected it. I know that my situation is incomparably different, but I feel like my desires and unmet expectations echo Jesus' heart's expression in the moment of His most frustrating and deserted hour: "If there is another way God, I want something different, but I trust that who I am becoming through your guidance and my obedience is always best." (Journaled the day I turned in the first rough draft.)

At some point, this book somehow switched and sadly became more about what it would answer and how it would represent me. This was so far from its sincere beginnings as a way to help people with a similar story in the hard moments. I became more focused on my imperfections and weak answers than His perfect love and truth. This is where I have gotten discouraged and wanted to quit.

I grew to loathe and love this book because it represents exactly the stage of life I am living and still learning. There is so much more here that can't be expressed in a few pages, but I'll sift and sacrifice to at least make sure I share the twenty percent of gold I have found in the midst of hard. And it's still an incomplete story that I have to let go of at some point, and say this is all I've got for now. If there's still more, there will have to be another chance or next time. God, please turn the great moments and incompletions of this book and me, from a less than complete sacrifice to a worthy gift through the power of Jesus…through the power of one who can make miracles out of my mistakes, and whose strength is made perfect in my weakness.

Thank you for those who never gave up on the vision to help us twenty somethings, in an often neglected stage of life and in a season where many mistakes happen out of desperation and loneliness. God, help us to turn and run to Your help because that is where our salvation lies, and will always lie everyday that we have a choice.

Introducing Young Adulthood

Have you ever thought to yourself, "What in the world am I doing right now?!?" Yeah, me neither. It is crazy being twenty something and feeling like my place in this world is still undecided. You would think that God and I would've figured this out by now.

Sometimes life is great and sometimes it's awful. Sometimes I am certain about life and other moments I second-guess everything. Sometimes people get me and sometimes they don't. Sometimes I want recess back and other times I want to fast-forward ten years. Sometimes life is simple, other moments, it's impossible. Sometimes I like people, sometimes I don't. Sometimes I love going anywhere whenever I want, and other times I long for consistency. Sometimes I think I should have "life" figured out, and other times I meet seventy-year-olds who don't. Sometimes I feel like I have nothing to offer the world, and other times I feel like I have everything.

That's where I start. There is a rising need for voices to speak up about life in the twenties, especially unmarried ones. I feel alone, but deep down inside I know that I can't be the only one. I long for answers and being understood. I long for people who know exactly what I am going through. But who will understand? Where could I have those conversations? What answers do I even want? And as easy as it may sound for others to help, the truth is that plenty have tried and I just wasn't satisfied with their answers…so here I am today.

A good amount of the answers you want can't be found in this book because they are situational and related to your future. Where should I be living? Who should I marry or what type of person will fit me best? What work will make me truly happy? How do I get the success I want?

This book can't solve all of your major problems, that's what the Bible is for. This book can't give you all of life's hard answers, that's what a relationship with God is for. This book is not designed for me to become rich, famous, and popular; that is what good looks are for.

I'm twenty something, unmarried, and out of school, what an awkward place to be! I am so awkward, churches don't know where to put me, authors don't know how to write about me, and I don't even know how to deal with myself. I'm as awkward as that unexpected zit that just appeared, with no quick solution or sign of leaving.

Why is it now, when I arguably have the most freedom, least amount of responsibility, and greatest chance to pursue my dreams, that I am still lacking something? And what is it? I have friends, but few solid answers. Who can truly understand me and take the time to help me figure this out? You may feel differently than me, but at least take comfort in this: *You are not alone.*

My Story

I grew up in San Diego, California, loving sports and being outside. I was carefree and loved my life growing up, especially when I didn't have to think about my future.

Life stopped being fun when I was told I had to look ahead and decide on my next steps of education or career. The stress of the future got to me. Thankfully, right after graduation I found a job that looked *ideal* based on my past: California location (I moved from California to Indiana for college), by the beach (I'm a surfer), good starting salary with benefits (security sounds good), with a great setup, office, and low responsibility.

The only problem was this trifling hunch that God was pointing me to uncharted territory in a small country halfway around the world instead of toward security. Where did New Zealand come from? It was one of those uncanny times where New Zealand just kept popping up everywhere in different life situations. I was passing the same billboard every ten feet. The random unexpected placements were too laughable and outspoken to ignore, and I couldn't escape how alive I felt inside when I thought about the opportunity.

Sounds exciting, sounds awesome! Except... turning down the ideal first job with benefits, receiving two amazing job interview calls the following week for jobs in the US, and earning minimum wage at a grocery store, before heading overseas into the complete unknown wasn't exactly how I envisioned myself putting all my education to good use. I still remember the day I was pushing grocery carts and laughing out loud at myself earning minimum wage less than a mile away from that other perfect job and paycheck.

So I started the New Zealand journey, nervous, excited, and ready to explore. It was going great until someone would ask me what the life plan was, "The life plan? Eesh! That all went out the window when God led me away from chartered territory, secure money, and the easy planned course to success! Now I'm kind of taking it a month or year at a time. I'm just trying to figure out life right now…let alone what the long term path to success looks like!" This was really hard for me to stomach at first, but experience soon taught me to find comfort in this: *the unknown is a normal part of life.* We are all bound to face the inner and outer feelings of embarrassing red-faced "uh oh" moments when we take risks for our true passions.

Few Answers

Less than a year later I was twenty-three, back from my overseas adventure, and expecting to have more answers, but I didn't. The odd thing was that neither did my church or culture back home. They were short on clues. They were equally confused outside of suggesting the typical American dream that wasn't working for me: work harder, find a steady good job, build security, and build a family so you can sit back and live well later hopefully. Is that it? Not that this solution is even bad, but is that the only answer out there? Even if I am not completely ready for a family or season of grunt work just to earn money, these are my only responsible choices?

Now I am twenty-eight years old, I have traveled more than I thought possible, achieved more life goals than I ever knew I wanted, been blessed to have lived with five different families and watch how they live, worked the gambit of jobs from sitting behind a desk to outdoor instructor, and done my best to love people well while avoiding regrettable selfish decisions. I've moved multiple times and I'm still uncertain where I will settle down more permanently.

I have only dated three girls seriously with no relationship officially lasting longer than four to six months. This means I have been single for over twenty six of the twenty eight years I have been alive, so I definitely know what it means to be single.

I don't have it all figured out, but I have been very intentional about trying to live this stage of life well… to grow and squeeze every ounce of experience out of this lemon called life.

If I was asked what I hope to be remembered by or what I would want my tombstone to say, it would go something like this: *Brent lived life to the full. But it wasn't just for himself. His life centered around loving others and God, that is what made it full.*

Trail Marker

What a lot of us miss, or at least I am missing, are not our hidden desires and dreams, but the trail markings letting us know that we are still doing okay and heading in the right direction instead of just walking in circles. We long for a reference point and place to go.

The cool part is this: the path we are walking down is not untraveled and overgrown with weeds. You may decide to trail blaze off the main path, but the marked trail for singles in our twenties is delightfully more traveled and cleared than you would expect! I hope that my life can become a trail marker for you. That expressing some of my big life questions will help you to recalibrate, and find the beginning or arrows you need, to experience confidence that you're walking in the right direction with purpose.

Are You Ready to Change the World?

Can I propose a ground-shattering idea? Do you know why the twenty somethings are so impossibly hard? I believe it's because your life choices between twenty and thirty years old are deciding the trajectory of whether you will change the world like Jesus or miss the earthly Promised Land.

God's people were held responsible as adults for decision making, contributing, and participating in war around the age of twenty during their desert season.[1] And up until thirty, and not a second sooner, God decided that the perfect and most mature person to ever walk this planet was still in his developing and preparation stage for changing the world. Your choices from ages twenty to thirty are the x factor.

God's going to lead you into a desert journey in your twenty somethings with surreal mountaintop moments and valley seasons. This is the testing ground to see if your makeup is quality world changing stuff that will stand the test. Many choose to let their faith buckle under the pressure in this hard waiting season by throwing tantrums, careless parties, and compromising their character in times of weakness. [2] Others hold so firmly to their faith by thriving on God's presence, that strongholds will come down, and ground is watered even through their hard seasons of tears.

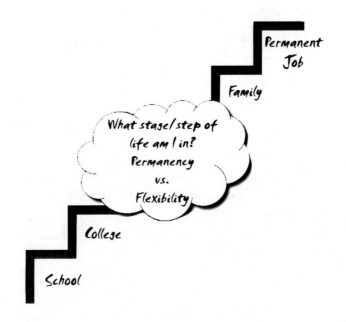

Are your twenty something's choices setting you up to impact the world as Jesus did when he turned 30 or not? It's a hard proposition, but this is your first chance as an adult to decide.

Are You in This Journey for God or Yourself?

Your reactions in the hard and risky times expose whether you believe the journey towards God is worth more or less than yourself. How committed you are to your wants versus God's will is quickly revealed when life gets too hard. Fun, comfort, and risk are put on the line, and you will choose to either complain and compromise your beliefs in the heat of these moments, or proclaim and commit your faith deeper. Which one are you doing?

Harder Than I Thought

Hi, hard. Who invited you? I prepared for a difficult game of paintball and got sent into an eight-year war with actual bullets! People warned me that the twenty somethings were hard, but they didn't express *how* hard. I learned something though while dodging bullets and running for cover: *everyone gets stuck in the war of hard.*

Righteous or unrighteous, good or bad, on the right path making right choices or not, everyone eventually gets stuck. I bought into the lie that I could avoid the effects of hard or stuck by doing the right things and I was wrong.[3] In a rush to get out and do, I turned the corner of adulthood and accidentally bumped into hard. It unexpectedly threw my organized plan up in the air, and I am still trying to recollect those pieces, wondering if I am too late or if I'll still be able to make it in time for my adult destiny to change the world.

I wish someone would've drilled the list on the following page into my head to prepare me for the typical hard moments that everyone faces, no matter how right or wrong we live. Hopefully then, I wouldn't have been so caught off guard.

The Typical List

- There are going to be multiple moments that I'm scared witless, and severely questioning myself and everything that I am doing, even while I'm on the right path.

- There will be multiple moments, even on the right path, that it's so hard I will feel like quitting it all. Just being done.

- When I pursue my dreams, I'm going to continually hear hurtful jokes and comments, even from people who love and support me but just don't understand.

- I'm bound to face the inner and outer feelings of embarrassing red-faced "uh-oh" moments when I take risks for my true passions.

- To achieve dream success, there will be temporary heart-shattering setbacks that I have to overcome in the middle of an otherwise great life.

- With a worthwhile direction, I'm going to face someone who sincerely and adamantly believes I'm doing it wrong and will publicly oppose me.

- I will never have enough time, money, or life experience to do things as perfectly as I could.

Shooting Straight Typical

Why weren't these typical hard moments more straightforward in the Bible and people's warnings growing up? Why did I need another book to tell me that *everyone* faces dips, before I realized this was a normal part of life? I never saw it coming, the intensity of life. But I don't know how I could've been warned. I mean, even Jesus' disciples weren't completely ready for everything.

God is a God of Those Who Say, "If only Jesus Were Here..."

I've been tempted to think that I'd rather have Jesus in person like the disciples did rather than the Holy Spirit. I feel like life would be easier to follow and more defined with God as a person leading me. But would it?

The disciples didn't always feel completely safe with Jesus around,[4] enjoy doing what Jesus asked,[5] know how to do what Jesus commanded,[6] or know where he wanted them to go.[7] Sometimes the disciples had no clue what Jesus was trying to tell them.[8] The disciples didn't always know if they would live and felt scared for their lives while Jesus was around.[9] There were times the disciples were too afraid to ask Jesus questions.[10] Jesus sent his disciples out into trouble like "sheep among wolves."[11] Everyone didn't get healed instantly with Jesus' authority,[12] and not everyone changed their ways when Jesus himself warned and told people how to find God.[13] Maybe the real issue to solve is not whether the Lord's presence is just as real and alive in us through the Holy Spirit, but whether our unmet human expectations and reactions are just the same way as the disciples were toward Jesus? We thought He would fix everything we want Him to right now, but He doesn't.

If Jesus didn't meet all of the wants and expectations of His disciples with His physical presence, no amount of God's presence is going to satisfy my attitude now, when I believe He's supposed to meet all of my wants and expectations right here on earth (which was really what I was assuming). Jesus actually says it is to our advantage He left and sent the Holy Spirit.[14] I sometimes need to kill my wants and unmet expectations to trust God as my provider in the hard times. Hard, unanswerable moments still come, with God by my side.

This is Life: Deal With It

You can't avoid hard as a human. Deal with it. Not only some hard. More hard than you and I ever invited, or wanted to be a part of our life's prescription. And when life is hard, it's hardly funny sometimes.

When life is hard, people are my happy release. I know I will always enjoy life because people are unavoidable and I love meeting new people. But I have always wondered how people who say they don't like people, enjoy their lives. Do they just tolerate living here on earth with all these "annoying" people moving around them? People aren't going anywhere, so it's probably smart for all of us to work toward enjoying others a little more than less.

This concept turned into a list. A list of "The Unavoidable Things Here on Earth That We Better Learn to Love or At Least Appreciate Because Otherwise We're Going to Be Miserable" ...a very concise title

I know. Can you guess what one of the other top life unavoidables is?

Hard.

Hard in unavoidable.

What do I mean by hard? My definition of hard is: an extremely intense difficulty that will shape you for better or worse.

What I really mean when I refer to hard is less of a definition or description and more of an experience. Meeting some people just can't be described in words. No matter how many words you use, they will fall short and pale in comparison to the experience... you just have to meet this person for yourself. Meeting hard works the same way. It is much more than a definition, it is something you must meet and experience for yourself.

Hard is where the problem eats up hope. It's where hope can't be felt, but must be trusted. Hard is when there is no easy answer. Hard is where the textbooks stop and the keys can't be found. Hard is often unexpected or impossible to completely anticipate. It leaves you questioning your survival if you run at it with everything you have. Hard affects more than just surface emotions, it taps in deep.

Hard is a brick wall. There is no easy way around it. Hard has few answers and leaves many questions. Hard is a lonely place where you wonder if others feel the same way. When trying to make it through hard, you realize it is extremely awkward and intensely emotional. Many who look at this wall want to give up because hard is large, heavy, complicated, unpredictable, and seemingly impossible.

When you run full force into hard like a brick wall, there are bound to be effects. Hard is a catalytic moment and season.

No one can escape being affected by hard. Everyone is affected by hard but not everyone wants it. So even though meeting hard is more of a description, the best starting definition is: an extremely intense difficulty that will shape you for better or worse. The question then becomes what do we do with hard when it comes?

If the purpose of hard in our lives is toleration just long enough for us to get through the difficulties, our lives will be one big disappointment. It's not as much about *getting through* the hard as it is who you're *becoming* through the hard. Life is more about who you're becoming than where you are going. Hard is not always right or wrong, but who you become is.

There's merit to the idea that life isn't so much about waiting for the storm to pass, but learning to dance in the rain and play in the mud. The decisions I make in this season will matter more than the season itself.

God cares little about the hardship or problems He can fix instantly, in comparison to us becoming more like Him and His heart in those hard times.[15] If we focus so much on getting through the hard without focusing on becoming more like Him, we have entirely missed the point. We need to work more towards God than our current goal.

It's essential to grasp: it's not as much about *getting through* the hard as who you're *becoming* through the hard.

Perspective Changers

I believe this book will be transformational for your life, even if you only develop this end practice of perspective forming. Henri Nouwen, who is a favorite author of mine, proposed that the simple practice of prayerfully repeating phrases from God's words like, "The Lord is my Shepherd I shall not be in want,"[16] three times will naturally enlighten and realign our hearts with God. [17]

I want to challenge you to develop this discipline of reflection by prayerfully reading the perspective changing phrases inspired by scriptures at the end of each chapter three times in an unrushed manner. After you read it once, take a deep breath, close your eyes and after you exhale prayerfully repeat the phrase again between each full breath. Or at least just read the phrase again two more times at your own unrushed pace. I promise you won't be disappointed with what you put into this. Let it marinate and soak in.

In this world you will have trouble[18]

The Young Adult Tango

I find it easier to dance by myself.

Yes, I'm the guy that loves to put on music, and dance in front of the mirror all around my empty house. Even though dancing close to someone is a great feeling, I am more myself when I dance alone. There's no pressure to perform and no experience needed when there's no one across from you. There are less expectations.

This is how many of us approach being a young adult. I would rather *just* act young or *just* act like an adult. But life complicates everything by putting these two separates together and forcing them to dance as one.

"It's time to live up my life experiences before I get too serious into commitments." Wait. "No, its time to settle down, pay off debt, and move forward in life." It's so much easier to choose one or the other instead of trying to make these two opposites get along and dance happily.

Young. Adult. That is what I am.

But as the saying goes, "It takes two to tango." We are caught in a dance where the push and pull between two forces are supposed to work together and move as one. I hear two very different but common stories from friends. Some strike the perfect job or relationship and make a secure life for themselves right away, and others have their life plan hit the fan, and can't quite figure out which direction is forwards and backwards. Is one of those options better than the other? Or is the grass really always greener on the other side? And are we completely responsible for which outcome happens to us or is it often beyond our control?

My twenty something friends are all over the map, but I can't shake the feeling that there are similar struggles we all are facing. But if that's true, where are all those answers from our combined efforts to help each other out? And where are the people with those answers?

I long for some direction from healthy young adults: someone who is embracing or has embraced not only the youngness of their twenties, but also the adulthood. Someone who knows how to dance!

Healthy role models like this are *extremely* hard to come by and our generation needs to step up and start filling this gap by being the living examples needed for the next generation to follow. We need to stop dancing by ourselves because it's easier. Let's show the world that although pushing and pulling resembles a fight, it also can represent the perfection of a purposeful dance.

Young

In one ear I hear friends emphasize the "young" in young adults. "Brent, you will never have a chance to travel like this again. You're only in your twenties? That's young! Don't be so worried about settling down with a woman yet," or "That sounds exciting...I think you should just do it" (in response to my latest and greatest idea). These encouragers play a crucial role in my life, but I seriously wonder if they ever consider the repercussions before getting caught up in seeing my life's potential as a wide-open adventure. On the other hand, there is truth to their advice.

I can't feel bad about not having it all together yet. And if I do have it altogether, I am far ahead of everyone else in their twenties because we are all still *young* adults. We shouldn't already know how to properly manage all our finances, get out every stain, cook every meal, make every dollar, manage every minute, fix every problem, kick every bad habit, get everything we've always wanted, and make everyone happy because we're only a quarter of the way into our lives and we would be way too cocky if so. We would have nothing else to learn or do! And besides, one big life lesson I have already mentioned is that we will never have enough time, money, or life experience to do things as perfectly as we could.

We can't feel guilty for the freedom that comes with this age. The energy and mobility we have without having to wake up at three a.m. to take care of three kids, and the ability to pack up and leave in a minute's notice requires no apology. This can be seen as a gift, and that is okay. This is a different life stage with its own pros and cons, so it is not something you have to apologize or feel insecure about, even if others don't see your freedom the same way.

We live in a culture of workaholics. We are expected to work seven days each week. Not even God Himself would ask that. Actually I find God telling us quite the opposite in the Bible. *At the beginning of time*, when God was setting up how the world works, He rested on the seventh day of the week and set it apart as a day of rest.

If you look at the Sabbath as an intentional day to rest and worship God, a day to sit back from career work and enjoy focusing on Him and what He's created, essentially God has asked you to take fifty-two days off for spiritual vacation and worship each year! That tallies up to seven-and-a-half weeks of resting from everyday work! I am definitely overdue a few spiritual vacation days this year, and the real kicker is it's my own fault! This shouldn't even be a guilty pleasure or splurge, this is what God desires.

Yet nowadays people argue that we are "freed" up to work seven days if we need to because life is "too busy" and we are no longer bound by the legalism of old rules. An endless life of work weeks with no rest is not freedom! Yet people and cultures succumb to a pressure all the time to work more than even God Himself has asked and consume more caffeine to keep up with busier lives than God has ever intended.

For those of you who are living around workaholics, there is a need to defend the practice of being young, restful, and playful a little *more* than less. So if you have the ability to travel or the flexibility to freely take a month off when you ask, appreciate this season. Don't feel like you have to apologize for being young.

Adult

In my other ear, I hear a lot of people who completely eliminate the "young" in young adult, because they fear that people are just shirking responsibilities and given an excuse to prolong immaturity. "Categorizing someone as a *young* adult just gives them an excuse to slack off. It's time for people in their twenties to just grow up and stop avoiding adulthood."

Interestingly, most of these comments come from people who got married straight out of college, or soon after, and never went through this stage of life themselves. Their view completely underestimates and labels a large number whose circumstances are beyond their control. They are actually where God has intended for them to be, instead of their situation being a product of laziness and avoidance. On the other hand, the lack of single men in their twenties stepping up to the plate, and media portraying the twenties as a party boy lifestyle has not helped in shattering the validity of these stereotypes.

My Journal at 23 Years Old: Hard to Understand

One of my biggest frustrations are friends who try to disregard this stage as *whatever*. It is almost guaranteed that the person expressing this was not single for the majority of their twenties. I have tried to hear these people out, but they just don't seem to get it. It bugs me that I have rarely or never heard the same arguments from someone who has legitimately lived as a single through their twenties saying the same things. They see the situation differently. There is purpose in the single twenty somethings rather than simple avoidance.

One pastor was asked, "You've talked a lot about twenty somethings today living in a sort of extended adolescence. Why do you think that is?"

"I think, in particular, it's the young men. Perhaps to some degree it is the young women as well...It used to be you go from *boy* to *man*, and now you go from *boy* to *guy* to *man*... It's just extended adolescence, where 20s, 30s, sometimes even in his 40s, doesn't really want to get married, doesn't really want to have kids, doesn't really want to pursue a career. He has a lot of hobbies, got a lot of buddies, watches a lot of porn, gambles, has a lot of fun, maybe plays in some band...or something ridiculous like that...

Those guys tend not to go to church. If those guys do show up at church, it's usually just to find a couple of gals to break the commandments with. And the Church doesn't really know what to do with them, so the least likely person in America to go to church is a guy in his 20s who is single... I'd say it's nothing short of a crisis, it's a real *problem*." [19]

This paints the perfect picture of a very real danger in today's culture. But while I read this, I also thought, *this guy obviously didn't go through this stage if that is the way he approaches the situation.* It turns out this guy got married in his early twenties. This does not mean that he can't impart wisdom and point out problems, but it does mean that he would have a harder time finding redeemable purpose for single men in their twenties when he never wrestled through it himself. Do I want to embrace this time of twenties and being single? Yes. Is it tempting to just act like a total screw up? Yes. But I also know that there are a number of single guys truly trying to live out their twenties well. The media doesn't glorify it, but they are there.

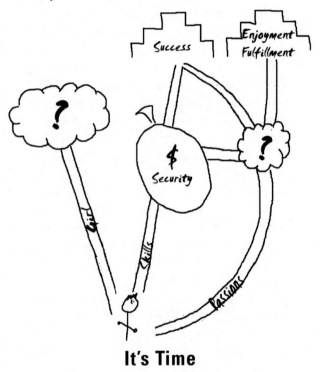

It's Time

It's time to start growing up a little more than less. Education and money have been poured into our lives for how long now? Too long. Teachers, parents, and the government have poured into us for over twenty years in hopes that we are "the bright future." It's probably time to start becoming that potential.

What this does *not* mean is you having to achieve *the dream* in your first ten years out of high school to be a success. If that is what you want, then go for it. Get a good job, get established, get your nice house, car, and spouse and start building your career, family, and house for future security. You can do it.

Yet any healthy adult can testify that *just* getting a good job or *just* getting married or *just* signing yourself into a mortgage, doesn't guarantee or automatically help you grow up in a healthy manner. There are too many people that are over their heads in debt and not growing financially responsible or secure with house payments. The divorce rates are horrible from people getting married without weighing the commitment they thought they would grow into. Having kids can motivate you but it doesn't guarantee you turning into a mature and responsible parent. It is not the job, house, kid, or spouse that makes you responsible; it is the growth process. So it's not necessarily time to enter parenthood, but it is time to start becoming an adult.

God is a God of Works in Progress

God desires *growth*. Otherwise, God would've had us all coming out of the womb at forty years old! You have hopefully been taught by now to be a lifelong learner. Well, I propose that you should be a lifelong grower and preparer. Each day, each situation is preparation for something bigger God wants to do through your life (Ephesians 2:10). Whether it's training for the next time a bigger challenge presents itself, or the day you worship God in heaven, life is definitely preparation.

One of the best parts of a relationship is living the journey together. It is not enjoyable traveling with somebody who's always telling you what you're doing wrong, but it is fun being around the people who stretch you to go places you would've never gone by yourself. This is God. He knows we are works in progress on a journey of preparation. Jesus was once a five, fifteen, and twenty-five years old Himself. He understands growth and knows how to walk the journey with us. He is the one that makes things grow (1 Corinthians 3:7). He is the one that will carry us to completion until the day of Christ Jesus (Philippians 1:6; 3:12-14).

Don't let embarrassment keep you from trying. Ask God to help or send you a helping hand. Be open to how God asks you to stretch yourself. Allow God to help you grow. Prepare.

Maturing Instead of Stepping Into Adulthood

Let's be honest, there are mature quality teens that I would choose to be like, over some adults I know. The first step in becoming a responsible adult is not finding adult-like security as quickly as possible to put our parent's minds at ease. Maturing is growing up, not acting grown up. Maturity isn't faking or acting like we are as established as our parents who have a twenty-year head start.

Although managing a house, family, and security can help you mature, it's the preparation, relationships, and drive from these experiences, and not the responsibilities themselves that bring maturity.

Do you know how to put your head down and do grunt work when a situation calls for it, even if you don't want to, like taking care of a baby in the middle of the night when you're exhausted? Are you willing to look past yourself and learn what it means to take care of your current family base when the excitement level is low and the quit factor is high? Are you willing to take a good honest look at yourself and change if you are wrong, much like a working marriage would require? Are you taking responsibility of how much your words rub off on others in the same way that a two-year-old will learn and repeat whatever you say out loud? Do you know how to prioritize your most important needs at the cost of smaller wants? These are some of the bigger questions of maturity that family and adulthood force you to grow into.

The first step in becoming a responsible adult is to know that you are not past learning, growing, and preparing now that you are out of school. Your best life approach is striving and learning through experiences right now, because this will make the biggest impact for you later. For the vast majority, it's said that your most effective and fulfilling work years will be in your thirties and forties, not your twenties. But we think, "We are young and ready to go, my prime is now! Now is when I have the most energy, friends, and can show the world what I can really do." Be careful. You can miss a huge part of the growth process if you try to skip a big growth spurt without learning the necessary lessons first.

Our twenties are when we are finally released to focus on the dream we have been preparing for so long. In our eagerness to do, we often fail to recognize that the major work is still not what is done *through us* at this stage, but what is done *in and to* you in this stage. Too often, people are looking and striving for what they want to do and accomplish, while overlooking and ignoring what they are becoming. Even though it is finally time to start living out your life, understand that this is also still a time of training.

Joseph is a great Biblical example of this. Joseph prepared until he was placed into position at the age of thirty.[20] He went through so many of life's challenges before God got him to the place He ultimately wanted him. He was Pharaoh's secondhand man and literally helped save a nation, including his family in the middle of a huge drought. Yet he had to endure so many trials along the way to maturity: sold into slavery by his own brothers, falsely accused of cheating with his boss' wife, put into jail, and forgotten about, after helping another cellmate get out of jail. Just imagine if Joseph would have given up on God in those years of waiting, training, formation, and maturing... It is time to patiently focus now on maturing into the adult we want to be in the future.

A Ten-Year-Old Senior Citizen

One of my friends said, "Sometimes I feel like a ten-year-old senior citizen." That makes so much sense! So young but so weathered. We are trying to act so much older and feel so much younger than we really are, or vice versa. God designed us to rest one day a week and to work six days of the week. God designed us to both be and do, to be productive and not productive some days. To play and work. Sometimes you have to ask a child to act older than they are and a senior citizen to act younger than they want. I am not here to argue what that looks like, but to agree that God wants us to enjoy being both old and young at heart, to be young adults. Dance.

Perspective Changers

Let it marinate and soak in. Repeat three times:

**Be happy while you're young...
follow the ways of your heart**

**But know that for all these things
God will bring you into judgment.[21]**

Why Don't Twenty Somethings Fit in the Box?

I don't fit in the box. I've come to grips with being a plastic triangle, but I still feel like I'm being pushed into the circle hole of a plastic box. I get the tension of the young adult tango, but I'm also having trouble squeezing into other people's boxes, including my own.

This is something that I don't know will ever change. People will always have unsaid boxes in life, and it's unnerving when something or someone doesn't fit. In fact, with a worthwhile direction, we're going to face someone who sincerely and adamantly believes we're doing it wrong and will publicly oppose us because of this.

My current twenty something's path isn't fully traditional, logical, ready, or charted. It's unknown. And this can frighten people...including myself.

Outside the Box: Nontraditional

Let me paint the scenario for you. At this point in your life you are about one of four who are still single in your current life stage. You are not alone. As a Christian single, you are about one of eight by my estimation. That sounds a little more lonely, but still not like a complete disaster.

I was traditionally taught in my culture that normal is getting married in your earlier twenties. Add church into the equation with all those Bible characters getting married in their early teens, tack on my friends' weddings, and I am starting to feel behind. I am a part of a new and growing group of people that history hasn't seen before. Not world history, but culture's history in a way that I don't fit in the culture's traditional box of still being single.

Outside the Box:
God's Nonlinear Side

Some cultures run on more of a linear thinking. From my best understanding this means that when A=B and B=C, it forms a line, which is the path you're supposed to take because it's the shortest path to the answer which makes the most sense: A to B to C. People will even conclude: since it's the shortest path to the answer it must be the *right* way to every conclusion. Take the straight line there. It's always better.

But if you are looking at your life right now, you laugh because you *know* it is not making the straight line you assumed it would. Beyond that, you and friends have tried almost every imaginable solution to put yourself back on that line and it still hasn't happened. You are now having this strong inkling that maybe life won't ever fit back on to that line you once imagined.

Good news my friends, God is above linear thinking. Linear thinking is not the only way. It has a counterpart and God created it too! It's called cyclical thinking and, to be honest, it doesn't make complete sense to a lot of linear thinkers. Cyclical thinking says, you will continue on a journey in circles until you come around to the same spot, but just further along.

For those of you that just want to get back on to the straightforward path of linear thinking, it is possible with God. Better news for the rest of us who see no hope or sign of a linear life happening any time soon is that this doesn't mean our lives are wrong or an automatic failure. Nonlinear doesn't mean you are instantly off of God's plan for your life. God is bigger than linear thinking. Detours add depth.

God never put a specific date or age on your marriage and dream job. I've checked the Bible and it just isn't there. God could've taken the Israelites on a straight line to the Promised Land at any point, but obedience was walking in the desert for forty years… And God was no less with them or leading them.

You might think, "Well, those people sinned, and they were disobedient and are paying consequences so that's different." You might be too! And obedience in the desert still means to follow God's lead. Even if you're not being punished, obedience still means following God through the tough times. And sometimes linear thinking is not God's intended path, even for the obedient. Have you ever looked at where God took the Israelites in the desert?

"When Pharaoh let the people go, *God did not lead them on the road* through the Philistine country, though that was *shorter.* For God said, 'If they face war, they might change their minds and return to Egypt.' So *God led the people around* by the desert road toward the Red Sea."[22]

To God, the shortest way is not always the right way or how He promises to lead. [23] We do ourselves a disservice when we take God's idea of a straight path too literally instead of acknowledging God's emphasis on His leading presence. Having life completely spelled out and logical past the point of needing faith was never His intention.

Lessons From a Blind Approach

I asked an extraordinary husband and wife who are both blind and have been married for over thirty years, "If you were to step into a new room or place you didn't know, how would you navigate through it?"

"If me and my wife were to go down to a hotel and walk into the lobby and we are looking for the front desk and we don't know exactly where that is, we may take our canes, and we may use our ears and noses and feel what's under our feet to take in the environment and move around in there…

It makes sighted people nervous. (Wife's interjection: If people think I am going the wrong direction, people feel like they *have* to come and help me).

But really there is nothing wrong with making a mistake. There is nothing *wrong* with finding something that isn't the front desk. It might be a flowerpot or a couch. All that information is still useful because you catalog it as you're walking in the front door. You're checking out things…"Well, okay so here is the couch over here, and the escalator and a stand, and there's the front desk because I can hear the printer going…" So finally you get a mental picture of that place. But if someone just grabs you by the arm and just hauls you from the front door to the desk, it deprives you of gathering all that useful information.

So, if you've graduated from college and go to work a minimum wage job for three months, despite feeling like a dreadful experience, it was a useful experience because you learned something about life that you didn't want to do for the rest of your life and it was still valuable information. It was valuable spiritual information, because you now understand what others experience where they may feel trapped in those scenarios. The moving around and gathering experiences are not wasted times, they are not useless."

Detours are valuable learning experiences. A detour from the quickest path of least resistance doesn't automatically define the path as wrong or wasted. One of the reasons you don't fit into the box is because your life doesn't reinforce culture's linear thinking as the only right way.

Outside the Comfortable Known Box: Single Twenty Somethings

People are getting married later or not at all. This is a growing trend but not in every part of the world. In any case, it is a different addition to culture that is already changing the way we do community. More single people are feeling displaced and alone.

Where this group fits into the social and work structure is still unsettled and this freaks out the traditions of many because it's change. I cannot predict where the growing single twenty-somethings shift will land, but the family culture and structures are changing. The unknown, uncharted, and untested leave too many loose ends for the practical mind to feel at ease. It's still too unsettled and means possible change. Another reason you don't fit sometimes, is simply because you don't nicely fit into people's defined comfortable box. Your stage of life is unknown and unboxable.

Out of Shape Box: I Don't Want To or Can't Wait Anymore

Sometimes when you find yourself restless, walking through a desert season long enough, history shows that we aren't too faithful as humans. If I was being brutally honest, a lot of my friends just can't keep their pants on and wait until marriage.

Either, we didn't learn how to hold on to our character through hard times growing up, or we just don't care anymore. We demand that He takes us back to an easier life and throw careless parties and tantrums to cope when life's too hard because we need a break from our spiritual accountability. Our self-control problem is bigger than sex, but sex represents our culture's insatiable need for the *now* feeling and our undeveloped discipline of delayed gratification.

We start to feel restless and insecure about whether we'll make it when we aren't able to land the job our education and work ethic deserves and we begin asking, "When is my time?" Other times we're just missing the companionship of a girlfriend or boyfriend, and it makes it so easy to question ourselves and ask why?

The majority of problems young adults face comes from an impatient lack of gusto to hold on to God and our character in the tough times when it's so easy to doubt and be unfaithful…and yes that is exactly what it is… doubt and sin. You are not going to be settled if you are not living right. A fourth reason you don't fit in a box is that you aren't completely trusting God or completely "in shape" yet to truly live right and finish the race you've started.

Underlying Why We Don't Fit

When my friend Evy paints a picture, I am amazed at how many different layers he puts on each canvas. His starting pencil sketches before he even paints blow me away. He starts with a pencil outline sketch followed by some base paints. He continues to add countless layers of oil paint with some final touches. It bugged me that I could've hung his intricate pencil sketches at the beginning on my wall with pride, but now they were painted over and will never be seen or appreciated by anyone. I was torn though because the finished project was such a masterpiece! This chapter is only a pencil outline on the canvas of this book to help us build the perfect picture. We don't fit into the box, so what do we do?

Perspective Changers

Let it marinate and soak in. Repeat three times:

**You do not belong to the world,
that is why the world hates you.**[24]

Alone & Unknown in
the Twenties

Why am I so scared? It's like I'm running through a pitch-dark forest with some unknown danger prowling around. It's crazy how the unknown starts playing tricks with our minds. I freak out when I realize safety is uncertain, or there's no one who can protect me. I am stuck in the unknown, all alone with unseen pressures, and no idea what they could do as they close in.

Alone and the Unknown. These are two recurring themes that I just can't get past. Whether chosen or not, there are going to be multiple moments that we're scared witless and severely questioning ourselves and everything that we're doing, even while we're on the right path.

Laughably Frustrating

Have you ever had one of those days where you stepped outside and wondered what the weather was thinking? It's somewhere between sunny and raining, and you're not sure whether it's misting or spitting. Or it's between raining and snowing and you're not sure whether to call it hailing, sleeting, or slushing? Sometimes I'm not sure there is even a word to describe the weather outside of *temperamental*. That's exactly where the single twenties stage of life is once you're outside of education.

Right there.

Right where you don't know quite what to call it, and what it wants to be. It's no man's land. Right where you react by smirking and shaking your head, or by getting just plain upset at the weather for not making up its mind.

Stuck Alone in the Unknown

School gives you direction and a social life but what do you do once you're out? Culture says, family and a good job answer this question. They will fix those feelings of alone and the unknown. They are security.

But what if you never left home or don't want to move back home or get married? And what if I can't get a job or my current job definitely doesn't make me feel more secure about enjoying life and my future success? Does that make me stubborn and selfish? Does that make me completely alone and lost? No.

But these questions do leave a lot of people feeling lost and confused. It leaves a group feeling alone like the invisible minority displaced in the confusing unknown shadows of mainstream…

Alone. You are not alone. We have all been there.

Unknown. You are in the unknown. But that is okay.

The unknown can seem like a lonely place. Like you're walking alone into a dark valley all by yourself instead of walking beside God through the sunny green hills like you imagined. Yet God is the Shepherd who's beside us through both the pastures and the dark valleys in Psalm 23. Why is it that I forget to picture God walking beside me in the valley of the shadow of death?

And why is it so dark? Why does it feel like He is not leading or protecting me when I can't feel his guiding staff? Some seasons can appear more scary or frightening, but it's important for me to remember that I am never alone if I have God. "We forget that we were never promised a twenty-year plan of action; instead, God promises multiple times in Scripture to never leave or forsake us."[25]

Stepping into the Unknown Together is More Fun

A few years back, I went to a multicultural performance night in New Zealand where I was pulled out of my seat five minutes before the start, and I was asked to give a greeting in English for the white European cultures. The only problem was that this was a crowd of a thousand people, and every other greeter had a tie or dress on and I was wearing a T-shirt, shorts, and flip flops in true surfer style.

I got up there with my casual welcome, including a "what's up," and I got a chuckle. After everyone said their different greetings, we were leaving the stage and without warning the host stopped us and said, "Now, we are going to have the Fijians, Koreans, Samoans, and Brent all lead us in a chorus of this old hymn in their native tongue." First off, I loved that I had now become my own nationality! Not American, not European... Brent. Secondly, not only did I not know the words but I also didn't know it was going to be sung to the British melody instead of the American tune. Great.

And of course I'm handed the microphone as the first to lead off... *Of course.* The crowd, the singers, and even the band are all looking to me at this point, waiting for my cue to lead off the song that I didn't know and was in no way prepared to sing. This awkward exchange went on for a whole year (but really like fifteen seconds) before they finally realized I was completely useless. The host cued the keyboardist to start playing while I mumbled my way through half of the words I didn't know and no screen to help. Finally, I stepped off the stage laughing out of emotional exhaustion and relief.

The crowd had no clue the amount of stress I had just undertaken by jumping into the unknown. They just saw a casual nervous guy. They didn't hear me praying, "God, that one was completely for You because there is no way I would've chosen that embarrassment for myself."

That is why I was so glad to have my friends who came with me sitting in the front row. They knew I had no intention of being on stage and understood the ridiculousness of what had just occurred. They were the ones that pointed at me with surprised, shocked smiles when they realized that instead of leaving my seat to go to the bathroom, I somehow had ended up talking and singing on stage! They were the ones that laughed and shook their heads with me as I sat down. Stepping into the unknown together makes it more fun so let me laugh at the unknowns of this season with you.

God is a God of the Alone

God puts the soul in solitude. Sometimes you need to just go up to the mountain. The mountain was a key place in the Bible where people met with God. It is important to make a habit of finding your own place of solitude, your own Garden of Eden or Gethsemane. Is there something special about that physical spot? Maybe not, but your personal expectation and desire to meet with God are reason enough for Him to show up. Church is a place you should be able to experience this with others, but hopefully there's a place where you can also meet with God alone.

Sometimes you need to go away to be refreshed. There is something about this intentional effort and struggle that God honors. What's one reason why youth respond so well to camp messages outside of complete physical exhaustion? They simply got away! There is significance in stepping out of everyday life to make time and a place for God. A favorite quote of mine is, "Nature is good medicine." The same theory applies. Getting away from a focus on humans and the world we've naturally constructed, unloads a pack of heaviness and distractions.

Sometimes you need to get alone to realize that you're not alone. It sounds funny but humanity can be lonely without God. We can have people all around us and still feel like we have nowhere to turn. Elijah is being chased after an epic stand for the Lord and complains, "I am the only one left, and now they are trying to kill me too," (1 Kings 19:10). God's reply is just as epic, "Go out and stand on the mountain in the presence of the Lord…I reserve *seven thousand* in Israel," (1 Kings 19:11,18). Seven thousand others! And Elijah thought he was the only one. Elijah had to go to the mountain so that his lonely soul could hear the Lord whisper what he couldn't feel or see, "You are not alone."

Closing the Gap Confusion: You Are Not Alone in the Unknown

You are not alone in the unknown. Just as acne and awkward haircuts inevitably go with being twelve years old, whether you choose it or not, you're already signed up for certain emotions and moments as you walk through the twenties. One inevitable is the temptation to feel alone.

There is a gap.

There is a gap between knowing what is normal in the twenties and what is portrayed in the media, and this confuses people. If all we do is hear writers, or stats about people in their twenties having a horrible life, how do we know whether it is depressingly true for everyone, or just that person relating and reinforcing the feelings of their own life with their friends? Is it really that bad? Or is it as great as those other single people say that this is the best time of their lives? It's near impossible to know what is real and what is the media. This truly is a confused and lost generation.[26]

This gap is precisely why I am writing. Where can an everyday person in their twenties realistically express the extremely hard unforeseen moments, which are a part of this season, while still painting the amazing picture of the twenties single life in all its glory? Can some normal people step out with answers of what life should look like?

I realize I can be adding to the noise and just as guilty of applying the personal experiences I've seen and heard to the masses, but I have to give it a try. I love being single and could stay here a long time, but I also could love marriage if it's in my life's cards. Hopefully, wherever you are, you will be more excited to share with me, that our experiences and feelings are more common than we imagined.

Perspective Changers

Let it marinate and soak in. Repeat three times:

None of us lives for ourselves alone, and none of us dies for ourselves alone.[27]

I'm Scary Emotional & I'm Not Sure I Can Tell You

Why didn't my emotions warn me that they're so jacked up? Up and down, up and down my emotions go. My nervous excitement builds as I climb up the big rollercoaster for the drop. The drop makes my gut tighten and scares me to the point of wanting to get off, laugh uncontrollably, and scream with that sick fear of wanting more. My instant contradicting emotions going absolutely haywire in this season of life, feel just like that rollercoaster and they scare me.

The hard emotions are so scary I'm not sure I can explain it to you or anyone else without feeling embarrassed. So scary I'm not sure you will be able to fully comprehend, feel, or be able to handle what I am about to express without freaking you out. Do you know the feeling I'm talking about?

The Develop"mental" Stage

I don't know why, but sometimes my actual life forgets to communicate with my feelings about how things are really going. And in return my feelings keep forgetting to give me a fair warning before things are about to go haywire without any real logic. There's a short in my system somewhere that's really emotional for absolutely no reason at all.

Let's just call it a develop*mental* stage. It's this growth spurt where I'm enjoying developing and growing so much while being left worried that I am way too close for comfort to going completely mental. It is like being on an emotional rollercoaster. I can be leaving my office whistling and excited about the accomplished day and as soon as that office door closes behind me switch into a momentary depression, wanting to cry and runaway from the world.

What is wrong with me? How did that happen? Honestly, I don't have straight answers. All I know from experience is that most singles in their twenties seem to go up and down emotionally a lot more than you would think is normal or healthy. Even for those who are pretty stable, it still happens.

I still fear that expressing the intensity of the following journals could hurt my credibility as a stable source, but I believe the need for others to know they're not alone is of infinitely greater value than my credibility on this issue. You know exactly what unexplainable and inexpressible intenseness I am talking about. You have been there or you will. You just may have never heard anyone else admit they have experienced the same frightening place or realized it was normal. There will be multiple moments, even on the right path, that it's so hard you will feel like quitting it all. Just being done.

Emotions Journal # 1:
The Emotional RollerCoaster Journal
(at age twenty-three)

In one journal I wrote:

> It's been tough. By other people's standards or view. I am sure my life looks manageable and glamorous, but right now, it is just plain tough.

This makes me feel like I just don't have room to complain or express myself. I know I am not alone on this one either. (This last line is me trying to coach myself rather than actually having an example that comes to mind to prove my point, but below is a picture of how I am feeling. I feel as though I am complaining sitting on top of all of these blessings and that there are other people who seem to be so much happier and content with so much less, so who am I to ever complain to or express this inner turmoil?

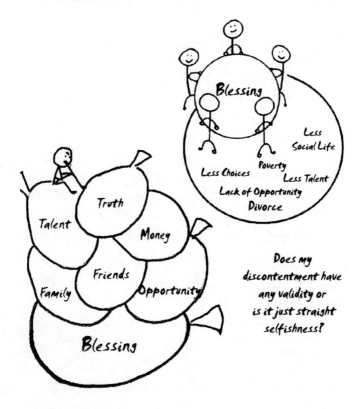

Blessing

Less Social Life

Less Choices   Poverty

Lack of Opportunity   Less Talent

Divorce

Truth

Talent   Money

Friends

Family   Opportunity

Blessing

Does my discontentment have any validity or is it just straight selfishness?

Yet, however small I tell myself these emotions or complaints are in my head, they still feel big. Huge. Like I am carrying the weight of the world on my shoulders or maybe better put, carrying the weight of life. Some days I come home feeling completely exhausted, emotionless, and feeling completely lazy because I accomplished very little by a *worker's* standards. On the other hand, I feel pooped because I feel like I have just carried the weight of the world on my shoulders all day. Whether it was responsibilities in my life that I am trying to figure out, or whether it is stupid circumstances that get me down or whether it is someone else's unfair life, or whether it is just trying to figure out how to honestly live out, and enjoy this crazy thing called *life,* I am just tired. I go to bed with a million things that I didn't do with the hope and exhaustion that I will wake up tomorrow with a new fervor and focus that doesn't replicate this moment.

I need a friend to get me going, I need that five-hour cleaning spurt that comes out of nowhere, I need that deadline that makes me go without sleep until I get the job done. Or I just need to be told that nothing needs to be done and it is okay for me to just sit back, relax, and know that life is okay. What do I do now? Where do I go from here? If I sleep, am I just running away or is this the sleep that God is rewarding me with for my life of contemplation and searching?

Emotions Journal # 2:
I Don't Want to Commit Suicide, I Am Just Done with Life.
(At age twenty-four)

Today is the day that I think to myself, "I'm done." I just don't want to do anymore. I am tired, life is too much, and I just can't do it. I quit on life.

Sooner or later, a person or obligation comes up and gets me off my butt when I am in this state, but I have become somewhat familiar with myself here. It is such a weird place to come to because I am a positive person. I wonder if my friends would freak out and think I am suicidal when I don't feel that I am. Other times I freak myself out and wonder: *Is this a suicidal thought or am I just frustrated? I'm definitely not really thinking about how to kill myself, but I am expressing emotionally the feeling that I don't want to move forward anymore.*

Emotions Journal # 3:
You Don't Understand How Bad It Really Is! (At age twenty-three)

Emotions are so hard to explain! I have these seriously intense times…I mean *intense* times of fear and gripping despair inside where I want to just cry, curl up into a ball, and hide from the world until it goes away or just stops for awhile.

The hard part is this feeling can come on me at random times and places, although it is mostly when I am alone. I don't think it is depression. I am not normally depressed and I don't really have suicidal thoughts. I just sometimes think it would be a lot easier if I didn't have to deal with the world. The worst part about these times is that they are nearly, if not impossible to share with somebody. Unless a person is actually there when the emotion overtakes me (which wouldn't happen because it only happens when I am alone), they will never be able to grasp its full power. I can talk about the moments of worry, feeling scared, and not wanting to deal with the world, but words don't explain that moment. Plus when I describe it to a friend, I can always downplay the intensity when I sense the friend is feeling out of place, worried, or awkward. If I explained this in its full extremity, I feel like most of my friends would think I was suicidal or depressed and be scared for me. Does anyone see past my normal interior to the person that is screaming inside of me?

Don't take me for a spaz, but there have even been past times in church where I can't explain my emotions but I have just wanted to run out of the church service screaming for no logical reason. There have been days in all of my ambition that I have wanted to just yell out loud, "I can't do it!"

The truth is, although this is a big problem inside at the time, it goes away over time. I don't know for sure, but I have to believe this feeling is somewhat normal among other single people trying to figure out life.

Usually, this means I have taken on too much or I haven't given myself enough down time. But who knows the reason for being in this place? All I can tell myself is this. "You have purpose. There is a reason God has you alive at this very moment. You may not feel it, but even if all you did was lay in your bed for the next few days and tell everyone that came in to see you, 'I love you,' you would be sharing God's love and fulfilling a part of the reason God has still given you breath."

Intensely Emotional

So how do you deal with this season of life that is so driven and dominated by emotions? It is a different level than normal. Your emotions are not only up and down. They are *intense*. They seem beyond what you can explain to someone else. What do you do with this?

I shared three journals but there were countless more. They are not fun to revisit as I read them, and I can't help but look at myself and ask if it was okay or healthy. Yet at the same time, if you know me or knew me in this season, you would've known that outside of this inner emotional turmoil, I was still a very stable man who loved God and worked consistently hard in my other roles. Suicidal or depressed? I would say no, but only by the grace of God. Intensely emotional? I would say most definitely yes.

God is a God of Those Who Want to Give up

"God, just make it all stop!" You were not the first to pray this prayer. Did you know that there were at least five Bible characters who told God it would be better for Him to just end their lives now if their current situations weren't changing anytime soon?

Elijah has just called down fire from heaven and made one of those legendary stands for the Lord. Afterward, in the loneliness of being overwhelmed and attacked he says, "I have had enough, Lord...Take my life"(1 Kings 19:4). Jonah gets so frustrated in the aftereffects of saving a whole nation that he says not once but twice, "O Lord, take away my life, for it is better for me to die than to live" (Jonah 4:3,8). Moses is carrying the burden of the Israelites grumbling on his own and says to God, "If this is how you are going to treat me, put me to death right now" (Numbers 11:15). Job. Good ol' Job. Talk about being alone. Everything is going wrong and even his best friends and wife are giving him bad advice. You know he's not happy when he says, "...I prefer strangling and death, rather than this body of mine. I despise my life" (Job 7:15-16). Last but not least, Jeremiah preaches God's message for twenty-three years, *twenty-three years*, with no visible results (Jeremiah 25:3)! In the midst of this trial he said, "Cursed be the day I was born! May the day my mother bore me not be blessed! ...Why did I ever come out of the womb to see trouble and sorrow and to end my days in shame?" (Jeremiah 20:14,18). If you have ever felt this way, then you are in good company.

Elijah, Jonah, Moses, Job, Jeremiah…these are not obscure characters! These are God's faithful men feeling alone and ready to quit. Yet God answered and was faithful to each one of them until the end, "for though a righteous man falls seven times, he rises again…" (Proverbs 24:16a) "…we are not of those who shrink back and are destroyed, but of those who believe and are saved" (Hebrews 10:39). You are not alone and God will answer and pull you through. God won't give up. That is why we are thankful that He is the God of us those who sometimes want to give up.

The Failure Gut Check in a Dark Room

I don't ever wish pain on someone, but it is so nice sometimes to know that someone else feels your pain. A solid friend of mine described a scenario where she was curled up alone on her couch with that same failure gut check I expressed earlier asking, "What in the world have I gotten myself into?" I thought I was the only one who had experienced that. It is so freeing to know someone else gets you or is helping to carry the weight of your frustration burden.

Seasonal Depression

When you live in a place with winter, you become familiar with the idea of seasonal depression. People go through a depression due to lack of sunlight during cloudy and cold winters. They have sun deprivation. They either fight through it, go tanning, come up with alternatives, or have to move to somewhere sunnier.

I don't believe it's a proven fact that singles or twenty somethings are more depressed than other seasons, but I confidently believe it's not uncommon to experience a first time or unfamiliar season of depression now. I can guess why, but I don't understand. Every season of life is hard but why are so many people dealing with depression now? I am not saying it is good to be in a state of depression but don't let an all too common experience, trap you into being embarrassed, or feeling alone like no one understands. You are not a failure, and don't let this keep you down.

If you are wondering whether your state is dangerous or not, please call and visit a qualified counselor, or someone who would know how to get you help at least one time soon no matter what the time or financial cost. It's necessary and worth it. You need to be honest with yourself and get help if you need it. Amazingly though, a medical state of depression is something diagnosable more often in a matter of months or period of time rather than a few days. If you're at the end of your ropes, get help, but also realize that many of us go through bottom-of-the-barrel experiences that are a part of life rather than despair.

If you are still wondering if your state is dangerous and you don't know where to start, here are two suggestions. First, if you have gone as far as actually thinking out a suicide plan in detail, go tell someone before you act. Please. Do it now. Making a plan is a suicidal tendency and you owe it to yourself, others, and God to tell someone in person before you act. Second, if you still don't know where to start, go to a church and be straight up with them so they know the intensity and can at least point you to help if they aren't qualified. Third, you are most likely experiencing Son deprivation. No, that's not a misspelling. When the sun isn't out you have to get creative with alternatives in the winter and when you can't feel or see the tangible Son of God in your life you need to get creative with prayer, people, and Bible alternatives.

Don't Hide Yourself

This unexpressed or unexplained fear is causing more depression and loneliness than I can predict. Young adults are hiding and not feeling known because they fear the extreme emotions of their lives will be taken the wrong way.

Stop it.

Find someone and tell them. Or at least try. Even if it's simply pointing out one of the journals in this book and saying to a friend, "This is how I have felt for the last few months." If they don't get it, regroup and tell somebody else who does. Don't let the emotions eat away at you like a cancer.

Did you know that the Bible describes a moment where all hell breaks loose on Jesus and all His closest friends desert Him and leave Jesus all *alone*. [28] Jesus *alone* is not something you hear preached very often. God himself has felt your predicament to its fullest. Yet Jesus' strong statement of faith in the alone was this,

"You will leave me all alone. Yet I am not alone, for my Father is with me."

We are not alone. We are not that special. God never gave us the prideful right to think that we are above or below anyone helping us. Others can help if you will let them in. God can help. Choose someone who really cares, and if you don't have any friends like that, go to a church, or find a stranger who will listen because you deserve that. Pray out loud because God wants to hear. God understands our craziness. One of His qualities that stretches to the max is patience. When we are at our wit's end for an answer, that's when the Holy Spirit has room to give one. "But how can He give us an answer when we are still well supplied with all sorts of answers of our own?"[29]

Perspective Changers

Let it marinate and soak in. Repeat three times:

I called on your name, Lord,
from the depths of the pit.
You came near and said,
"Do not fear."[30]

Not Quite Permanent & Waiting in the Terminal on Standby

This isn't funny anymore. What's the answer? I'm tired of waiting and feeling like I'm on standby at the airport. The wait can be exhausting.

Waiting on standby can represent one of the worst or best days ever. You're either getting that free trip to an exotic place, or you're impatiently stuck waiting for possibly days in circumstances beyond your control. Exciting opportunities mixed with frustration. Not quite there. This is another description of hard in the twenty somethings.

Life Audibles

Life sometimes calls audibles on us. An audible is a change of play in football. It happens when the quaterback calls a play in the huddle, breaks from the huddle, walks up to start the play, and decides to make a last minute play change from the original plan. He makes the call without regrouping, which only leaves seconds for the team to readjust. Then, ready or not, he hikes the ball and starts the play. Unprepared or not relayed, this can lead to chaos if the play starts, and players misheard or don't know what to do with the quick change of plans. You'll have frustrated players if they were not well prepared or warned in advance that this could happen. This is how I feel about the twenty somethings:

frustrated and unprepared for the change of plans that I didn't personally call or prepare for. Being *not quite permanent* is one of life's audibles.

Unprepared for Not Quite Permanent

Not quite there and not quite permanent. What could've prepared us for this? A lot of us have gotten to this exact point unprepared by our life's teachers for the changed play calls, and we're left in standby looking around waiting for someone to make the call.

The Established Traveling Life

The only thing established in life now is that things are going to change. With people averaging ten jobs in twenty-five years it's more like we are living in airport hotels than small neighborhoods.[31] Life is more transitional now and since transition is a normal part of this season, it's important to be prepared for certain rhythms that come with this on-the-go lifestyle.

Life Plan Audible # 1: Multiple Jobs: Did I Do Something Wrong?

Either we haven't landed the job we wanted or went through a season where we struggled. Life pulled an audible on how quickly we originally assumed it would take to find the right job and settle everything in our crazy lives. We ask ourselves whether we did something wrong. Why didn't I find or jump into the dream job right away?

Job security advice that's been rested on for years about finding a solid occupation and employer who will take care of you for life is far more obsolete and uncommon. Having multiple life jobs is becoming the new norm.

In a transient world that relies on change, a person's job security relies on the people you meet and the books you read.[32] In other words, it's now about constant learning and new connections. Not only a developed skill, but an ever developing skill and social network. In a culture that is fast moving, the only job security is to be always learning and meeting people that will continue to give you opportunities as jobs change.

God is a God of Perfect Timing

God's timing is perfect. The God who put time and seasons into the universe knows how to help you orchestrate your life. He also "has made everything beautiful in its time"(Ecclesiastes 3:11). Wouldn't it be awful to meet the love of your life when you're five years old and miss the opportunity because you weren't ready? What about feeling sick to your stomach from eating too much and then seeing your favorite dessert? Timing obviously affects the wants and needs of your heart. What might sound perfect now sounds less than desirable if the timing is off. Since God's timing isn't the same as ours (2 Peter 3:8) we may be asking for things that we are unprepared for, or incapable of receiving right now.

There are also times where we feel hard pressed on every side. Like time is running out and we're trapped in a corner with nowhere to escape. Fear not. The God who split the Red Sea can perform your impossible escape. His promise to make a future way for his people, rings just as true for you today, "I will even make a way in the wilderness, and rivers in the desert" (Isaiah 43:19 KJV). When we don't see a way we will be tempted to falter, but the goal is to come out on the other side saying, "…I trusted in, relied on, and was confident in You, O Lord; I said, You are my God. My times are in your hands…" (Psalm 31:14-15 Amplified).

This is the God who not only perfectly timed your birth (Acts 17:26) but also the birth of his son Jesus (Galatians 4:4). So when you are asking for something, or find yourself in a difficult place, realize that the Lord either placed you there or allowed you to be there (in this time) for reasons perhaps known for now only to Himself."[33]

Life Plan Audible # 2: Inevitably Living Back At Home

Another unexpected life audible that often isn't planned is moving back home with our parents after we finally moved out. Many of us will end up moving back for another short or long season of our lives in this state of transition. This transition can be a great way to be cost effective and grow closer to your family, and it can also be a horrible way to avoid growing up. Moving back home can be a step backward, but it also is a wise step forward depending on your situation and reasons.

The more entertaining part is the tension that comes with living back at home after high school. There is no way around it. Sometimes it's very mild, but growing up brings a more independent attitude that will bring friction after being away. There is going to be tension. Parents want to love the child as a kid, and the child wants to be treated as an adult or vise versa, so ridiculous curfews, lazy habits, and different views of how you should live your life are sure to come.

As our support and social needs change in the twenties, it also becomes more difficult to find the relational support you need solely from your immediate family. There is a deep consistent support that only blood family can fill, but there will come a time where each child finds their *family* and support, just as much if not more, from friends and others outside of their parent's home as they become an adult. This is a need that I believe can no longer be completely filled by parents.

This social separation can be hard to express to parents because it's difficult to even put our finger on; we know we are being helped and grateful for our parent's

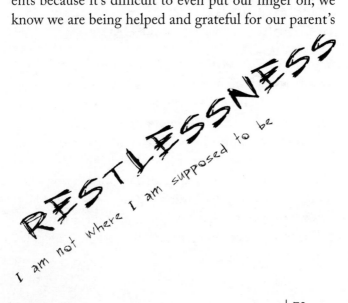

RESTLESSNESS

I am not where I am supposed to be

support with housing and food, but still feel unfulfilled. How do you express that your parent's love and time is so needed but just isn't enough because your main source of everyday support now comes from other friends or a special other?

Life Plan Audible # 3: The Two-Year Transition Give or Take a Year and a Half

Have you thought to yourself, "I am so tired of transition…or I can't believe I have to go through this whole phase of change and life searching again?"

Personally, I never imagined I would have to struggle through this whole soul search another three or four times before I was thirty! Going through the big direction change decision process so soon again was not in my original plans.

In the middle of my two-year trip to New Zealand, I met a guy in his early thirties who had just settled down as the owner of a Mexican restaurant. You may be so used to chain restaurants that this doesn't sound crazy to you, but Mexican restaurants all the way in New Zealand…that's a novelty! We were talking about this constantly moving season of life and he commented, "Two years seemed like a good time amount for me to keep transitioning, until I found this place where I wanted to permanently settle down for awhile." This made a lot of sense to me.

Whether it's moving locations or lifestyle job changes, you can expect a big life transition every two years, give or take a year and a half while you're still figuring life out. This is no math equation, but I am extremely impressed to hear a friend in their twenties who hasn't had a major transition happen within the last six months to three and a half years.

A Chance

Like a chance card in monopoly, you don't know if the result of your chance is going to be good or bad. You can never quite predict how the standby, terminals, or destinations are going to turn out and it can get old.

What you *can* control is who you are becoming through these chances. Who you are becoming is a choice, while what happens must sometimes be left up to chance (but really God).

You are either going to become a disgruntled impatient traveler, or a collected appreciative adventurer. You have a chance to either become a helper or hoarder with those traveling around you. You have a chance to be trapped in chosen loneliness, or strong in solitude.

A Chance to Be
Helpers Instead of Hoarders

I am not sure if you realize this but you have a once in a lifetime chance to help different people when you're in transition. We say we will help more when we have more money but now is the time. It's a random phenomenon. As we walk and live in transition, we find ourselves in unplanned situations. Alone, you often have chances to meet people that you would be too distracted to meet or notice with other friends around.

Room for One More?

It is amazing how I ended up in the right place at the right time, to give someone a ride or a few extra bucks when I am casually traveling. Being alone or single, I often have room for one more. Whereas in a group, my table is often "full" in my head.

Other times in transition, we acquire things that we don't need, or don't know what to do with, so we more often share. In certain traveling places, you will find boxes of random free equipment, backpackers just leave behind for the next adventurer. I wish we unloaded like this more often outside of the traveling scene.

I love my music, so it's no surprise that I have seen this most clearly in my life through the giving and receiving of music players (more specifically iPods). The process of giving and receiving something we love brings so much needed sacrifice and joy into our lives. Over the past five years I have gone through the giving and receiving process of an iPod *ten* different times. And they almost all directly point to God laying it on the heart of one of my Christian friends to be generous. Let me share one story of how I received an iPod when I was living overseas and lower on money. My friend wrote…

> I'm quite excited though about your iPod story. Here's the deal. I had to get a new laptop as the one I was using was on loan from my dad. They then gave me a free iPod Touch. I had an iPod, a really new one, and had no need for this one. I wanted to give it to someone

that may not be able to just up and buy one whenever. It's so weird that you just gave yours away—especially to someone who got theirs stolen. I had the exact same thing happen to me last summer—twice actually. I had mine in my car, it got stolen. As a going away present, I was given another one. That one got stolen. Then my parents felt really bad about all of it and got me a really nice one. I think it's awesome that you gave your iPod to someone who got theirs stolen and would love to give you this new one…Let me know where to send it if you would like it.

This message was sitting in my inbox as I gave my iPod away, but I only read it after I had given it up. It makes me wonder how many blessings God has sitting there waiting to be sent, just waiting for me to sacrifice and give first. I got the iPod in the mail a day or two before I headed back overseas again. It was another reminder that small gifts of love and sacrifice represent so much more.

I can't tell you how many times I have struck up conversations, or been able to help someone later at night in a restaurant or coffee shop because I was out studying, instead of home with a wife and kids. Transition can be seen as another death look at uncertainty, or as a gift and opportunity to help the people we unexpectedly approach. It all depends on how you look at it.

A Chance to be Strong in Solitude or Choosing Trapped Loneliness

We have all had that night, week, or month where everything is amazingly full of life, color, and people, only to be abruptly woken up the next morning to an eery lonely still. A place where all we're left with is ourselves and empty silence.

I remember distinctly waking up to a cold house after a month of spending all day eating out and showing new friends around my home city. The next thing I knew I was sitting at the kitchen counter in a dim chilly house listening to the silently loud crunch of a potato chip, peanut butter, and jelly sandwich in my mouth.

We all have those *back to all alone* days where we are stuck having to deal with ourselves and the feeling of loneliness. The moment is inevitable, but what you do with it is not. Will you choose to appreciate your alone time to rest and develop while seeking others out in true community? Or will you feel trapped in the loneliness, wallowing that there is no one around and scrounge for a distraction or random person to break the uncomfortable white noise instead? Are you teaching yourself the art of being comfortable with yourself?

The difference between alone and lonely is this: lonely comes when you feel trapped alone and it's beyond your control or want. It's forced. Solitude is chosen aloneness. It is appreciated and chosen time alone that is seen as intentional or a freeing opportunity to simply be. But even solitude can quickly be tainted by oncoming feelings of loneliness if we let it. Even when you're married you can feel lonely. Loneliness is not the absence of people, but the absence of being known and comfortable with yourself.

Some of my best times of developing a new skill and meeting with God are when I'm alone. Besides, there are some people that actually make me feel even *more* lonely when they're around. People can help, but they can also be my avoidance tactic.

Life can feel like you are sitting in that terminal seat, watching millions of people on a pressing destination walking right past you. Like the countless headlights of cars passing by me as I drive home alone represent life: full of people who will never know or have the time to reach out to you in your time of need. Or you can choose to explore the terminal and make friends with the person next to you, knowing there's someone in that terminal feeling the exact same way. You can enjoy the forced rest and pray for someone to stop, and help you enjoy the journey. Are you going to see your time in the terminal as an adventure or as being trapped in a glass box of emotions? When I was feeling restless and trapped during one season, my good friend Cathy rescued me out of my thoughts by saying, "I think, that until God tells you otherwise, find the exotic and exciting where you are... It's just waiting for you!!!"[34]

You can't always control the life audibles of *not quite there* or *not quite permanent* that leave you on standby. But you have a unique contribution in this transitional phenomenon to become a pleasant life traveler. You can become more confident to handle anything thrown at you, or more confused when life calls the next audible. And remember to keep hope because sitting in an airport terminal on standby means you might be one big breakthrough away from going to your dream destination.

Perspective Changers

Let it marinate and soak in. Repeat three times:

We are travelers passing through this world as foreigners and strangers.[35]

Purposed to Appreciate the Present on Purpose

Guess how many people have been single in their lifetime? 100%. Guess how many people have been married? Less than 100%. You may feel alone but the reality is that more people relate to you being single. Whether you are in the *single for life* or the *single for a season*, the truth still remains, you're single. And there is more than just a reason you're in this stage: there is a purpose to you being single. There is also purpose to your twenties. Let's get logical.

First, you can't skip your twenties just because you want to be in your thirties; it is just physically impossible. So God has a purpose for you waking up today in your twenties.

Second, if you have asked and believe in a miracle working God who gives good things to both the good and bad, you could already be married, but you are not…So God has a purpose for you waking up today not only in your twenties, but single.

Third, you didn't wake yourself up today. You were woken up. [36] God could've pulled the plug, and you could've died in your sleep last night, but He woke you up this morning because He decided there's purpose for you to be alive today. And therefore, I now know that you were at least woken up today, right now, for this purpose: to live *today* well as a single in your twenties until God says differently. You have purpose.

Stop before you read on. Reread the purpose sentence above once more.

Do you honestly believe there is a purpose for you today outside of feeling confused and moving backwards?

We know this in our being but sometimes it's just so hard to feel and accept.

This doesn't have to be your long-term life purpose. This is a part of your life purpose for right now. There can be a holy discontentment with the word *single* because you know marriage and family will be a part of your future. But, and this is a big *but*, if you always despise, and never accept living well as a single you are potentially setting a life pattern that's never content with the season where God currently has placed you. You need to be a steward of trusting and accepting *now* instead of avoiding it.

Your present situation is a gift from God. Moving all the junk and mistakes aside, God woke you up as a gift, not to punish you. God knows it's hard and He wants you to know that He longs to give you the pure desires of your heart. May he grant you your heart's desire and fulfill all your plans!"[37] He longs for you to have all the good that will help you to succeed and be a shining example of His love.[38]

Too often I get ahead of myself in the unguaranteed future. I tell myself today or tomorrow I will go here or there, spend a year there, find a life partner, carry on business, and make money. But I do not even know what will happen tomorrow. What is my life? I am only a mist that appears for a little while and then vanishes.[39]

Time is too limited to let the future worry us out of the present. What if we began to pause, and to realize that, maybe, this one moment, with this one person, is the very reason we're here on Earth at this time?[40]

"We steal if we touch tomorrow. It is God's."[41] I don't have tomorrow as a guaranteed gift, all I have is today, and *today* I at least know God purposed for me to live the twenties well as a single until He says differently.

God is a God of Right Now

God is Present. Now is the moment that He wants to be in your life. Now is the moment that matters. God lives in all of eternity, but He understands that our past is set, our future is unknown, and the only moment we're guaranteed to actively change is now. God is most concerned with who you are becoming today, because today's choices make you into the person you will be tomorrow.[42]

The Bible says it is unwise to ignore the future (Proverbs 6:6-8), but it even more clearly states that we have no guarantee what will happen tomorrow. "Do not boast about tomorrow, for you do not know what a day may bring" (Proverbs 27:1). "Now listen, you who say, 'Today or tomorrow we will go to this or that city, spend a year there, carry on business and make money.' Why, you do not even know what will happen tomorrow. What is your life? You are a mist that appears for a little while and then vanishes. Instead, you ought to say, 'If it is the Lord's will, we will live and do this or that.'

As it is, you boast in your arrogant schemes. All such boasting is evil. If anyone, then, knows the good they ought to do and doesn't do it, it is sin for them" (James 4:13-17).

What you have been guaranteed is *today*. Whatever is planned or unplanned for today, make sure that you're living in a way that you would gladly present it to God.

The Grass is Always Greener

I really do have to remind myself that the grass is *not* always greener on the other side. If you haven't had enough life experience to really believe this, it's true. When you believe there is somewhere you can move or someone you can marry that will fix everything and cure all your problems, you are blind.

There are better and worse places, better and worse people for your life but there is no physical place, person, or season on this earth that God has deemed spoiled and unredeemable. Whoever thinks a certain place or person is their problem is more likely the very thing that is spoiled themselves. We can't always change our circumstances, but we can change our response to those circumstances.

My friend so wisely put it, since you can't escape the world's problems by moving away, the answer isn't so much moving away from them as it is learning to manage your current problems to enjoy life where you are presently. In other words, instead of always trying to move to greener grass, life's about learning the art of enjoying and making the grass greener wherever you walk. [43] Too often, our attitudes have us standing still in one spot so long that we are actually the ones killing the grass, and expecting everyone else to move around and water the grass for us. We point at problems all around us that others need to fix to make our experience more enjoyable, while turning a blind eye to the dead spot of grass we're currently standing over and creating with blame, complaints, and ignorance.

If the grass is greener on the other side of the fence, fertilize your own. If we start by learning how to better manage our current problems, we will water and make grass greener wherever we go. We must participate in making green grass, not just pointing out where it should be.

If I know God's purpose for me today is to live *today* well as a single in my twenties until God says differently, then whether I'm choosing to accept or avoid that purpose right now will determine whether I am becoming a grass water-er or killer. It will determine whether I am watering and living in a state of paradise peace of God's trusted goodness or in a land of dead grass where all I see and point out are dismal questions and problems. One major part of finding paradise is that life is more about a change of perspective than a change of place.

Perspective Changers

Let it marinate and soak in. Repeat three times:

I wake again, because the Lord sustains me.[44]

Riddle Me This

Every time I try to simplify, I come up with a complex solution! Some twenty something's problems are like getting to the second to last note of a great song, and not finishing. It's as if there is no hope or anyone capable of finding the last note and our only fate is a suspended resolution without the resolution. It leaves a nagging insanity in our suspended minds. We are left begging for the last note to put our uneasiness to rest, but it's yet to come. This is how I feel with my current life problems that don't have an answer yet.

All at once, these life issues have randomly been popping up out of nowhere and there isn't really a resolving answer to be had! Although I can give answers to these problems, I'm not sure when, or if they will ever be completely resolved.

Can Single For a Season Be Okay, Please?

You've never dated too seriously, already been divorced, or just got out of a serious relationship. Relationships almost feel like *Russian Roulette* to you at this point. If you loaded a bullet into one of the six chambers, spun it, put it to your head, and pulled the trigger, you have absolutely no clue what the outcome would be but you wouldn't be surprised with your luck if it landed on the bullet.

That is why people who keep asking you if there is a love interest in your life can get so annoying. It either rubs salt in an open wound, or beats the dead horse that you don't even know how it died! Sometimes people have the nerve to joke about whether you are even attracted to girls or guys. Others try to set you up on a blind date. It all can be fun and helpful, but also embarrassing and full of nice tries. When we pursue our dreams, we're going to continually hear hurtful jokes and comments, even from people who love and support us but just don't understand.

You Can't Blame Them Journal (journaled at age twenty-three)

> You know I can't blame those who try and help. I mean there are times where I have been so appreciative of someone helping me find a job or possible date…But I appreciate them less often than they probably think. They are married and loving it, so I can see why they would want to pass that gift along. It's like a hidden treasure that they can't help but want others to find, but I'm just not sure that marriage is the hidden treasure that will make me truly happiest at the moment.
>
> I had a conversation that went like this:
>
> "Brent, you can't have your dad cut your hair, what if it turns out horrible and you see people you know at the conference?"
>
> I responded, "I have had friends cut my hair in college. I just don't care."

"But, Brent, what if this is the last time you see some of your friends for a long time?"

"I just don't care."

"Brent! What if your future *wife* is there?"

The truth comes out. That person definitely loves me, but at the moment they were just another person putting expectations on me from their personal life, about how to make my life better. It doesn't mean they don't care, but there are two problems with this: one is that they are putting expectations on my life about what I need, which I never wanted or asked of them. And two, they are assuming that I am at a place that is insufficient... that needs fixing.

Don't get me wrong. I see the beauty of marriage. I see how happy couples are together. I am glad for them. I know they experience something unique that I never will fully understand until I am married.

But seriously...I mean *seriously* seriously, what if I really just don't care about having a relationship right now! Is that really inhumane?

That doesn't mean I am not attracted to girls. That doesn't mean that I wouldn't love having the perfect dating relationship and girlfriend I was totally loving. But right now I just want to be. If a relationship comes, it will be right, but realize that this is a stage of life that I am in and it is okay. I don't need you to fix me.

Brainstorming? Yes, definitely... if I ask for the support.

Dreaming for me? Yes, definitely... as long as it is dreaming with me, but then supporting the decision I make, not the one you have decided is best for me.

I see so many friends settling down. Some are just settling. Others are really settling into living their dreams. I will probably end up with a steady job maybe even close to what they are doing, but I just can't settle for the normal secure family life right now. It would be settling.

I have different desires. I have different dreams. And despite not having the money or stability or security I will want at some point, finding myself in life experiences, and searching for what I'll pour my heart into is so much more valuable at the moment.

America is on a kick of success. It says, "The sooner you find your job and focus your life, the better you will be because, the more money you will make, and the better your chance is at prestige and fun." I'm not sure I buy into that. I don't know what it is, but I think this misses something. It may not be the complete norm, but I hope American culture leaves another place for the eighteen to twenty nine year olds not in college. The main two places of community I've experienced are either the party scene where you find your fun and fulfillment around beer and sex, or the security scene where you find your fun and fulfillment in marriage and responsible early success.

Where is the place for the rest of us outsiders? I live somewhere in between. I am not wanting to go trash my life, or throw away responsibility, but I'm also not ready to leave this different kind of freedom and excitement that comes from not living the family life. I want to live life to the full, but I don't have that girl. I don't have that job. I don't even have the direction. I don't have answers to even be fulfilled.

The conclusions I have come to so far: Life is better with God during this time. Life is better when I consistently catch up with my friends throughout the week. Life is better when other people help me reach the goals they can by coaching rather than telling. And when I remain single, this will always be an ongoing issue to some degree.

One ongoing question of the twenty somethings is wondering if I'll ever be allowed to be content and single free of pressure.

Is It Possible To Find Someone Of Quality Who Completely Relates?

Let's be honest, it can be hard to feel understood by some married couples because they did get married and can't completely do the same for us yet. One of the main reasons my twenty something friends often settle for a fling or less than ideal relationship is because they're in lonely times, feeling hard to understand, and desperately hoping to give love a chance.

We long for some comfort in the midst of feeling misunderstood and like no one can relate. Or we fear our lives are too boring and we just want to spice it up with a little fun. For whatever reason, what I do know is that forced relationships have caused a lot of damage. I see way too many friends who lower their standards for unhealthy relationships that result in impurity, regrets, breakups, and avoidable marriage problems. But the question keeps lingering, "Is there really someone of quality out there for me where I don't have to settle?"

Why is Everyone Dying on Me? Death and Junk

Another open ended and unexpected season is the increased amount of funerals and tragedy. Where did all of these unexpected deaths and people getting sick come from? There's a defining point where it feels like more hurt and death bombard our lives for no logical reason whatsoever once we get a little bit older. Maybe people tell us and we see it more, or maybe it's simply because people are getting older with us, but now our life problems seem to include way more funerals, miscarriages, tragedies, and divorces that are a gross part of life.

I remember reading a book in English class called *The Giver*. I hate books with sad endings, and this was one of them. The main character lives in a black and white world. As his teacher starts to open his eyes to another reality, color starts to enter in and enlighten him, but a curious thing happens. In the midst of gaining wisdom about the world the boy doesn't become happier. His life and world become weightier instead.

I like happy endings. This is not the picture of a happy ending I would paint, but there is truth in this idea of wisdom.[45] One of the unexplainable parts of aging and maturity is experiencing a different wave of life's heaviness.

Wait, My Parents Aren't Perfect?

Changing family dynamics are also characteristic of this specific growth season.

First off, let it be said that I have amazing parents. I couldn't have asked for a better home and upbringing. So why is it that we begin to question our parents so much after we graduate? For the first time in your early twenties, you realize parents can be wrong, sometimes if not a lot, and you begin to separate all the ways you don't want to be like them. You make statements like, "I will be different" or "I'm not like my mom or dad who…"

This is okay for a season and it's good to shape yourself by seeing what you don't want to be. But while this is good for awhile, over time you must come back and balance out that imperfect realization, with the fact that whether they succeeded or not, it's guaranteed that your parents tried to love you in their own way more than it's possible for you to ever know. The Bible talks too much about honoring your father and mother for you to risk doing otherwise. [46]

In many cases, I have had my friends end conversations about their parents with "my parents really aren't that bad." Which is really the truth; they are just processing their differences for the first time. This separation can easily come out as a negative towards the parents that they truly admire and love. Don't settle for recognizing their imperfections without learning to love them better, because those very characteristics have most likely shaped and taken root in yourself more than you know.

There's a growth curve in learning to accept the reality that the people you admire most can and probably will still hurt you and make mistakes as humans. But when you're tempted to get frustrated, remember that parents almost always, if not always, deserve more credit than their children can possibly give. I am constantly and consistently overwhelmed by the loving kindness and sacrifice of parents when I take in the total picture.

Am I Still My Parent's Child or an Independent Adult Now?

Another family change is making the relational switch, from you being the young child with adult parents to approaching your parents as one adult to another. If you haven't already experienced this, there will be a time where you have to play adult and address a family problem or misunderstanding and set appropriate boundaries with your parents in ways that you never anticipated.

Why Can't Life Be More Black and White?

Growing up is also when we test the areas of grey that we didn't while we were still under our parent's roof. It is the time we own our lives and beliefs in a different way. To do that, we often explore the black and white boundaries of what is good/bad, right/wrong, and innocent/harmful that we didn't push before. What we soon realize is that there are more greys in this world than anticipated. Some are not as bad as we thought and some are even worse.

Life isn't as black and white as we were told as kids. I believe parents and teachers are almost set up for failure here. As teens mentally grow and begin understanding things more conceptually, they hit a crisis of mistrust about what they have been told and how things were explained. But what could be done? Kids listen and respond to concrete black and whites like, *yes* and *no*, *do this* and *don't do this*. They are raised up on concretes because that is how they mentally process. But as they understand and comprehend life more conceptually (that problems aren't always solved as easily as 2+2=4, and that sometimes there are x's and trains thrown in) those kids began to question the concretes, and whoever taught them in such a simple format.

We question our parents and teachers but we are equally as guilty for filtering out what we couldn't conceptually understand up until this point, without knowing that's what we did.

Life isn't as black and white as it looks in the movies. I used to think life was more simple and that the answers I needed were more concrete than I do now. At the same time, I still believe there's truth in the statement: The Bible's commands are simple to understand, but hard to follow.

So this does not mean that I lack certainty, deep convictions, and concrete beliefs in my life. It does make me a little less anxious to jump out and force my convictions on everybody else.

This is not a new problem but it is definitely a heightened one in today's world. The clash of cultural differences with people traveling and the instant international conversation that happens online definitely leave people with more questions on what is black and white. Being a generation that is more okay with juggling contradictions also contributes to the confusion. Moving out of home and making your beliefs your own are a major contribution to grey issues hitting you in the face for the first time. This shouldn't surprise you.

Am I Doing Enough?

Am I doing enough?

This is one of the questions that can haunt you endlessly in this season of unknowns or for the rest of your life if you let it.

This one question alone can leave you in the dark if it is left unaddressed. I personally have had two extreme reactions to this question: there have been times I feel absolutely worthless and other times where I wonder why everyone can't see how awesome I am as God's gift to this earth. Both are honest. Both have hints of truth, but neither are the full picture.

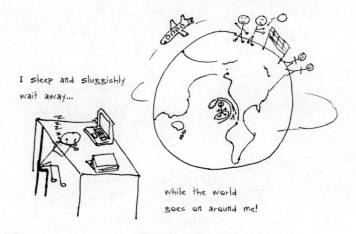

I sleep and sluggishly wait away...

while the world goes on around me!

Why Am I Worthless? I Have Nothing to Offer

There are times where I feel like I have nothing to offer this world. I traveled to New Zealand for seven months at the age of twenty-three to work and live. Life was simple in one sense, but there was about a three-month span where everything went wrong. I lost, broke, and failed at everything. At the end I said to myself, *What in the world do I have to offer? Seriously, I can't take care of anything I own or even take care of myself, so how in the world will parents trust me to work with their teens in the future? I don't even trust myself with their kids! How should I expect them to? I will break them, lose them, or fail at helping them.* It is a humbling place to come to rock bottom. It is devastating and it just hurts inside.

Why Can't You See That I Am God's Gift To This Earth?
I Have Everything To Offer

Then there are other moments where I can't understand why people just don't see how absolutely amazing I am!?! Don't they know that I am a rock star inside? It might be a turned down job interview, or a random conversation, but there is just this sense of wondering if people know who they are really talking to and what I am really capable of? If they only understood, or knew that I am made to do something great even though I do not know what that is yet, they would feel honored to be talking to me before it all happened. Not in an overly swaggering sense but in a hopeful sense. Okay, and maybe in a little bit of a cocky sense. I may not know everything, but maybe I will find an answer to solve some huge problems or make a big impact in this world…ya know?

I smile at myself even as I admit this, because we young adults are such a dichotomy! I know that this is cocky. I know that there are plenty of people smarter than me, more focused than me, and more capable than me that have set out to solve the world's problems, contribute to the world's wisdom, and come up with solutions and answers that have still failed to answer all of the world's questions or be revolutionary. So what do I have to offer? And then there is this other sense that there has been none like me, that if I am given the right circumstances and opportunity, something ground-shaking will happen through this unique snowflake! (That's what they tell you when you're five, right?)

Why Am I Questioned So Much?

Being questioned too much is draining. The worst part about making a bold stand in the unknown is that you are bound to be questioned and rightfully so because your answers are still somewhat unknown. So there is room for questions, way too many questions. We know this.

But understand, being questioned is one of our most defining moments in discovering who we are and what we stand for. It really determines what you are made of:

how much grit you have when people put you to the test and what qualities make up your core.

It is sharpening to fight through times where people doubt or question how you live and what you believe. At the same time, if the questioning is more accusing, remember that the enemy is the accuser and that he can often try to bring you down. One of his best tricks is stacking on way after way that you should doubt yourself, or feel like a failure. Don't allow this compiling trick to happen.

Part of growing up is facing hard questions and situations with no easy answer. Life is getting harder, so its time to equip ourselves to get stronger with it.

Small and Big Contributions

Your major contribution may look different than mine, but I believe you've had a similar dream. It will look differently for everyone. For some, this major contribution will be on a worldwide scale. For others it will be on a national scale, online, through their church, in their group of friends, or through a few close family members, yet whatever this groundbreaking idea is, its impact is sure to go beyond the direct people you influence!

And just so it is said, on whatever scale this moment happens, whether it is global or for one other person, it's not only making a difference, it's huge. Any task can be equally as important to God depending on what He has called and created you to do. All our different efforts can be equally needed and as impacting. I believe that a parent who pours all of their love into one child can be just as impacting as the president trying to love a nation. God is impacting the world while focusing on individual transformation at the *same exact time*, and we need to be okay with following suit. Nobody made a greater mistake than he who did nothing because he could only do a little.[47] Go conquer the world.

"I have often dreamed
Of a far off place.
Where a hero's welcome
Would be waiting for me.
Where the crowds will cheer
When they see my face.
And a voice keeps saying
This is where I'm meant to be.
I will find my way.
I can go the distance.
I'll be there someday,
If I can be strong.
I know every mile,
Will be worth my while.
I would go most anywhere
To feel like I belong."

-Hercules

Perspective Changers

Let it marinate and soak in. Read below three times.

If I am still trying to please men I will not be a servant of Christ.[48]

Unknown Hardships

Sometimes I just want to kick life right in the face. I'll be going through an impossibly hard time and I just can't understand why.

I forget about the word hardship in the Bible… not persecution for doing something right, or discipline for doing something wrong, but just going through hard for the sake of hard. Testing, tribulations, temptation, effects from an imperfect world, call it what you want, but hardship's definition is not just discipline for wrongdoing, but the whole training process of a child;[49] the training process that we, as children of God, go through our entire lives. Here is what the Bible says about hardship.

Understanding Hardship

You can think something's a hardship when it's not. Also, you can falsely make something a hardship out of selfishness when you are not thankful. "Do not consider it a *hardship* to set your servant free, because their service to you these six years has been worth twice as much as that of a hired hand. And the Lord, your God will bless you in everything you do" (Deut 15:18).

Hardship is a normal part of life that still seems big, even if it is our own faults: "Now therefore, our God, the great God, mighty and awesome, who keeps his covenant of love, do not let all this *hardship* seem trifling in your eyes—the *hardship* that has come on us, … In all that has happened to us, you have remained righteous; you have acted faithfully, while we acted wickedly" (Nehemiah 9:32-33).

God may lead us into hardship or trials, but He will always save those who hold on and never give up on Him. "God has besieged me and surrounded me with bitterness and *hardship*" (Lam 3:5). "Moses told his father-in-law about…all the *hardships* they had met along the way and how the Lord had saved them" (Exodus 18:8) "Who shall separate us from the love of Christ? Shall trouble or *hardship?*" (Rom 8:35)

God wants us to accept hardship as a necessary part of living right without complaining. "I only know that in every city, the Holy Spirit warns me that prison and *hardships* are facing me" (Acts 20:23). "We must go through many *hardships* to enter the kingdom of God." (Acts 14:22) "Now the people complained about their *hardships* in the hearing of the Lord, and when he heard them, his anger was aroused" (Numbers 11:1). "Keep your head in all situations, endure *hardship*"(2 Tim 4:5). "Endure *hardship* as discipline" (Heb 12:7).

Getting through hardship isn't the ultimate goal, it's love: "If I…give over my body to *hardship* that I may boast, but do not have love, I gain nothing" (1 Cor 13:3). "You have persevered and have endured *hardships* for my name, and not grown weary. Yet I hold this against you: You have forsaken your first love…" (Rev. 2:3-4)

God wants us to see hardship as our joint effort with Himself to do something amazing, not simply a responsibility to endure. "As servants of God we commend ourselves in every way: in great endurance; in troubles, *hardships* and distresses; …known, yet regarded as unknown; …having nothing, and yet possessing everything" (2 Cor 6:3-10). "This is why, for Christ's sake, I delight in…*hardships*…for when I am weak, then I am strong" (2 Cor 12:10).

God Knows Our Feelings

There's nothing necessarily wrong about the feelings and emotions that accompany our instant reactions to hard times. What can be wrong is whether we follow through with God by holding on to our character or not.

Jesus posed this story to a religious crowd:

"There was a man who had two sons. He went to the first and said, 'Son, go and work today in the vineyard.' 'I will not,' he answered, but later he changed his mind and went. Then the father went to the other son and said the same thing. He answered, 'I will, sir,' but he did not go. Which of the two did what his father wanted?' 'The first.'" (Matt 21:28-31). God knows that our instant response may not always be perfect, but He is patiently waiting to see who will follow through on what is asked of them, especially in hardship.

What Is Your Response to Unknown Hardship?

Do you still think there's a better plan than this hardship, and are you willing to stay where God has you if not? Are you using careless words or actions because you're tired and frustrated? To achieve dream success, there will be temporary heart shattering setbacks that we'll have to overcome in the middle of an otherwise great life. This season right now is a test of your true current state of faith and patience in God. This is what God says: "In quietness and trust is your strength, but you would have none of it. You said no, we will flee... blessed are all those who wait for him."[50]

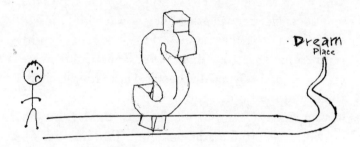

God is a God Who Has Everything You Need

God is Rich. What is a few hundred or billion dollars to God? He could destroy or create that in a second. God has got what you need. He can get you the job, plane ticket, salary, husband, car, house, or anything else you want in a heartbeat. And rest assured of this, if you are doing your best to follow Him, you have nothing to fear. God has got your back covered. "Some trust in chariots and some in horses, but we trust in the name of the Lord our God" (Psalms 20:7).

The question must be asked, though, if he doesn't give you what you are asking, does that mean he doesn't love you? If he decides not to give you what you want, will you still trust Him?

We often say, "But God wouldn't do that" or "I won't be happy with God unless ____ happens…" It seems that there is a question of submission first. The problem with submission is that it's testy! Submission is only fully tested when it goes against what you desire.[51] God wants to pour out His blessings, but He knows the emptiness His gift will bring if it is at war with Himself. If God is not at the center of His goodness, the gift can become your god. This is why some of the greatest verses on receiving always start with God. "Delight yourself in the Lord… and he will give you the desires of your heart" (Psalm 37:4). "Trust in the Lord…and he will make your paths straight" (Proverbs 3:5-6). "But seek *first* his kingdom…and all these things will be given to you as well" (Matthew 6:33 emphasis added by me).

First, come to God submissively, then, ask freely: "Bring the whole tithe into the storehouse, that there may be food in my house. Test me in this," says the Lord Almighty, "and see if I will not throw open the floodgates of heaven and pour out so much blessing that there will not be room enough to store it" (Malachi 3:10).

God's Hardship Is Not Always How We Picture It

Like the moment a different face is put to a person you imagined in your favorite book or on the radio, God's hardship throws us off when it looks different than what we assumed. We think we can finally wrap our minds around the cost of living that God asks of us to follow Him, but we can't. To be honest, I think this is one of the most frustrating lessons to be learned as a follower of God. It will always cost more than we know we can give. It will cost everything. "Anytime you try to move forward, there is risk. Even if you're doing the right things, your risk isn't reduced. But there is no progress without risk, so you need to get used to it."[52]

How Scary Can God Be?

There is this underlying tension that asks how scary can the almighty powerful God be, if He is good and loving? God is supposed to be as close as a father and caring as a friend, right?

We are okay with likening Him to an actual physical force or storm, like ocean waves or lightning, but we are not okay with likening Him to causing the same kind of damage and turmoil these forces would create in our daily lives. Those feelings are okay to look at from a controlled distance, like a caged lion at the zoo. But heaven forbid, God actually have the nerve to jump over the fence with His power, and scare us by being untamed or uncontrolled in a way that threatens our sense of safety and comfort.

It is all over the Bible. God is likened to powerful, not always pleasant forces. God is like a scary storm, earthquake, and fire.[53] A lot of times we dismiss the implications of these statements as okay to talk about as long as we are exempt from fully experiencing them. Otherwise, it might leave us feeling scared and not in control. But who said anything about safe? God isn't always safe by the world's standards, but He is good.[54]

Under God's Covering

One of the writers of our time had an interesting take on God's covering:

> In 1 Peter 5:6 it says, "Humble yourselves, therefore under God's mighty hand, that he may lift you up in due time." I felt like I was doing that. I was humbling myself under God's mighty hand. So why then did it feel like I wasn't making any progress? Why did it feel so dark? Why did it feel so uncertain?
>
> Because of my expectations.
>
> I failed to realize that sometimes being *under God's mighty hand*, can feel a lot like being in a cave. That's the reality of being under something. Have you ever been under a blanket? Or under a bed? You're hidden. It's quiet. It's safe.
>
> But it's not what I expected. I didn't want David's experience, where he retreated to a cave with his men and his God. I wanted the verse

to say, "Humble yourselves, therefore on top of God's mighty hand." I had a secret expectation of what it means to be protected by God and it didn't include the word *under*.

I also hadn't expected the phrase, *due time*. I expected the verse to read *your time* or *Jon's time*.[55]

God is beyond, bigger, more powerful, and more in control than all of us. He can and will take us through times of uncomfortable and frightening feelings. Feelings where He knows it is good and we don't. This will be especially hard for us who don't trust, when we can't understand. It's very easy and enticing for human understanding to believe a good God would never desire for us to feel extremely uncomfortable, and out of control in the unknown although this is untrue. That is our limited comfortable definition of good rationalizing.

God in the Dark

We might take the God analogy of light and dark too far. Sometimes I think God is more involved in some feelings we call dark than we want to admit. So unless we are going to start talking about sunburns that God causes as the light, let's not throw the baby out with the bath water, and fail to acknowledge God may be more involved with the hard, almost darker, times than we are comfortable owning.

Unavoidable Unexplainable Hardships

There will be problems that you will never understand why they happen. Your responsibility is to seek God more, and hold on to your character, no matter what, in these unknown moments.

Seeking God More

I had a mind-blowing moment one day. I realized that God asks for one consistent response no matter what or why I am going through a circumstance: seek God more. In each situation, God's attempting to show me His great power, and reveal Himself to a whole new level.

In the unknown moments that you just want to scream, "Why," or want to know whether you did something wrong to deserve this, or whether you are being tempted, or whether you are facing the consequences and discipline of your sin, or someone else's sin, your response should always be the same. Seek God more. Seek and lean into God instead of away from Him. Anger, lack of time, and confusion are the perfect times to press more into hearing from Him. There might be good times to ask why, but it is not always necessary to know. It is more necessary to hold on to the love and truths of God. Surround yourself with God's Word and others who will speak God's Words into your life.

Satan is trying so hard to get you to quit on life, when God wants you to keep going. Don't just keep going, keep going to God.

Miracle Abraham Faith

Twice, Abraham hid the full truth from kings about Sarah being his wife, instead of trusting God's protection. He was still learning to trust God when he couldn't see the outcome, yet Abraham's belief in God goes far deeper than most of ours ever will. When God said he was going to give his barren wife Sarah a baby, as they approached one hundred years old, he chuckles but trusts. When God tells Abraham to kill this very child which was promised and a direct answer to prayer, he doesn't argue or hide the command, and explain it away as something God wouldn't do. This time in his older age, he trusts that the miracle working God could raise his son Isaac from the dead even though he's never seen this happen.[56] Abraham trusted God to make the right call while he was obedient in the unknown.

In unknown seasons we don't always understand, we must trust that God will pull through in a miracle working way beyond our understanding. Our following must go beyond our understanding.[57] It's the only way to hold on to our character instead of justifying cheating the system.

Perspective Changers

Let it marinate and soak in. Repeat three times:

**You will find me when you seek me
with all your heart.[58]**

When You Don't Know Why...
Look to the Rubik's Cube

"You're not seriously asking for that, God? You are not seriously going to make me give that away?" Did you know that a secret to life is risk, and that a secret to life's risks can be found in the Rubik's Cube? The puzzle's genetics challenge us to risk everything to ultimately get to our end destination... finishing the Rubik's Cube. Life often asks us if we are willing to take the same risk. You will be asked repeatedly to see if you are willing to risk it all for God and your dreams.[59] You have got to mix things up to get somewhere.

The reason I love and hate the Rubik's Cube, is that it makes no sense from the outside looking in. It looks fun to try, until you realize you have to ultimately risk losing all your hard work with no hope of getting it back to keep progressing. Unless you decide you won't give up rebuilding and moving forward when you mess up, it is impossible to make any more forward progress. The only way you are going to solve the Rubik's Cube is to seemingly scramble everything up, and that's a problem for most of us! You are going to have to take risks, mess up, and seemingly move backward to completely figure out how to resolve certain life riddles. Sometimes looking like you messed up the whole thing is the best way to the end! We can learn a lot from looking at the Rubik's Cube.

Rubik's Cube Learnings

It took me six months to practice and truly learn the Rubix cube as a learning process for this book. Here were my ongoing reactions while trying to solve the Rubik's Cube. I think these reactions are very similar to our own in the midst of tough dilemmas where we haven't found an easy solution.

• It hurt my brain because I couldn't always see or compute exactly how it was going to work out… even with an answer's guide in front of me.

• The answers didn't just come naturally…actually, I looked at the puzzle and I just wanted to throw it against a wall.

• I am debating on whether my persistence should keep me going, or whether I need to put it down for the night.

• I lost my Rubik's Cube on day two and haven't had time to replace it…Also true of the unknown. I try and deal with life problems, and if I don't get immediate answers, life happens and fixing the important things often gets put off for way too long.

• Day two Reaction: "This is easy!" Day sixty Reaction: "Ha! This has taken way more work than expected and I'm still unsure I've got it down for good!"

• You have to trust the proven systems…when you can't see how it works out.

• Lesson learned: Life lessons and changes take more than a first time attempt to really cement in my life.

- One of the motivating thoughts that keeps me going is the hope or false belief that "a few more times and I've got this." Translated: Hope or the belief that I'm almost there. It usually takes a lot more energy and time than two hours, but persistent self-coaching that I'm making progress and almost there keeps me going!

- I naturally want to understand something to solve it. I started the Rubik's Cube with this desire, and still want to understand why the formulas work... over time. Although it's helpful, I'm realizing it's not necessary to grasp *why* a formula exactly works to be able to solve the problem. "You can understand more of the why after you know and have done the how."[60]

- There have been way too many frustrating times where I have gotten stuck. I've frustratingly moved backwards in the puzzle to a point where I feel like I shouldn't have to repeat or go back through...and each time I have to decide whether I will see this as a learning experience to solidify and re-solidify what I think I already know, or just quit and say, "I pretty much already know how to do it," while refusing to do the necessary grunt work of sharpening my skills to cement the answer in my life.

- This verse in Ecclesiastes 8:16-17, also gained deeper meaning: "When I applied my mind to know wisdom and to observe man's labor on earth—his eyes not seeing sleep day or night— then I saw all that God has done. No one can comprehend what goes on under the sun. Despite all his efforts to search it out, man cannot discover its meaning. Even if a wise man claims he knows, he cannot really comprehend it." Although all of the needed answers to life can be found through God, there's still an incomprehensible depth to explore. It is a limited comparison but I have also found this to be very true of the Rubik's Cube process.

God is a God of the Perplexed

God can leave us perplexed. God leaves Daniel perplexed with His interpretation of the king's dream, "Then Daniel was greatly perplexed for a time, and his thoughts terrified him" (Daniel 4:19). God leaves the witnesses of Pentecost amazed and perplexed; they asked one another, "What does this mean?" (Acts 2:12). God even left Paul and the church perplexed, "We are hard pressed on every side, but not crushed; perplexed, but not in despair..." (2 Corinthians 4:8). The common denominator in all these stories is God at work. At Pentecost, the perplexed reaction is a response to the Holy Spirit coming over the disciples. With Daniel, the perplexed reaction is in response to God's answer. In 2 Corinthians, perplexed is a result of Christ's figurative death at work so that God's life may also be revealed.

Definitions for perplexed include, "being at a loss; not knowing how to decide, what to do, or which way to turn."[61] Read that again. How true is that statement about our lives at different times? Other words for "perplexed" that came to mind as I was reading the scriptures were shock, disbelief, dumbfounded, doesn't compute, and only God.

Only God.[62] What a beautiful phrase. In an attempt to avoid doubt, I think Christians can be afraid to admit when we are perplexed. Yet these puzzling experiences are often radical moments where God has done or is doing something miraculous, dumbfounding, to which the only response is often *only God*. This may sound ridiculous at the moment, but don't be ashamed when you're perplexed. Get ready to be amazed.

What You Need To Know When Life Is Jumbled

The Bible's trusted patterns are there as a helpful guide, when we need to know the how before the why. You will seemingly have to go backward to go forward at times, like paying the consequences for confessing a lie to become truthful. When you've moved backwards, you can begin to grasp that the hard learning experiences are deeper than just extra unnecessary grunt work. They are the muscle building character moments necessary to set a solid foundation for future breakthroughs. Hard cements God into our lives.

You might have to lose a job, or quit something you love to create space for an even bigger dream to come true.

And just so it is said, even if you know the formulas and are trusting the God solution to make progress in your life, from the outside looking in, observers will think you are messing everything up when you follow this method. They can't see that sometimes you are less than a few tweaks away from the solution. We can't lean on our own understanding because sometimes we will only realize what God meant for us after the fact. [63] Your life plan will have to look jumbled to move forward at times. Are you willing to accept and learn this again?

Moving Backward to Move Forward

There are plenty of examples of godly people having to move backward to move forward. Gideon has to reduce his army to practically nothing to win. The disciples of the king of the universe were not sent out with tangible riches to change their world, but just themselves and a friend. Moses was born with a stutter instead of eloquent speech and was chosen to lead one of the biggest movements of all time. The disciples were left to watch Jesus die and sit in waiting for months to see whether they had failed or just moved backward to move forward.

Sometimes part of God's plan in the jumbled seasons of life is to free up space for God to do something new and miraculous in your life. God may have a purpose in you looking like you are backtracking. It's almost like you took a trip out to a viewpoint on your hike with God, which wasn't wasted time, but now you have to backtrack for a bit to continue moving on the main trail towards the top.

Perspective Changers

Let it marinate and soak in. Repeat three times:

Lean not on your own understanding.[64]

A Promised Land Perspective

One day, as I sat back in a recliner seat with my awesome little bib, my dentist asked me how my day was going. I said, "Busy, going hard, but having fun doing it." He said, "That's not what I would want." He caught me off guard, so the conversation paused awkwardly for thirty seconds, then I asked, "Well, then what would you want?" He contemplatively put his tools down, and after about five seconds deep in thought said, "Peace." Talk about an unexpected dentist visit!

I think the dentist was on to something. When I really thought about it, I concluded that I think we all desire a peace of mind.

Peace.

The *Promised Land Perspective* of peace that Jesus describes in the Bible is more about a change of perspective than place while we are here on earth. It's more about a change of purpose than problems. It's more about a change of person than power. This is the *Promised Land Perspective*. This is where you find peace.

More About a Change Of Perspective Than Place

Peace is more about a change of perspective than a change of place. This is why the Bible tells us to be transformed by the renewing of our minds.[65] How we view and see things will directly influence whether we find peace. If you look at the world through the wrong glasses, it will look wrong. Those who have a tainted perspective will not ultimately enjoy life inside, or outside of the Promised Land, because their spoiled nature spoils the place wherever they go. Your adult life choices have a shelf life that require you to focus on changing your perspective. Changing the physical place you live, or being placed in a different stage or season won't automatically change your perspective for the better. You could be in the perfect place and still have no peace with a bad perspective that spoils everything. This is something that will only happen as you go to God more in the midst of your current day and life season.

More About a Change of Purpose than Problems

Peace is more about a change of purpose than a change of problems. The Bible tells us that God's purposes won't fail although men's purposes will.[66] Those who have a tainted purpose will not ultimately enjoy life inside or outside of the Promised Land because they are set up to lose. Their spoiled purpose creates ugly problems wherever they go. Your adult life choices have a shelf life that require you to focus on changing your purpose. Changing the problems in your life, or moving past your current problems won't automatically change your purpose for what's right. You could get through every problem imaginable and still have no peace if you do everything for a bad purpose. This is something that will only change as you go to God more in the midst of your current day and life season.

More About a Change of Person than Power

Peace is more about a change of person than a change of power. The Bible tells us that power in the wrong hands will not be celebrated, and will come to nothing.[67] Those who have a tainted person will not ultimately enjoy life inside or outside of the Promised Land because bad power does not fulfill. Their spoiled person creates power struggles wherever they go. Your adult life choices have a shelf life that require you to focus on changing your person. Changing the amount of power or ability you have to answer, fix, or obtain your dreams won't automatically change you into a better person. You could have all the power you've ever wanted and still have no peace if you're unhappy with the person you've become. This is something that will only happen as you go to God in the midst of your current day and life season. It's your choice to begin.

A Promised Land Perspective of Peace

A *Promised Land Perspective* of peace is not about having nothing hard in your life. Peace is found through an ever-growing God perspective, purpose, and person in the midst of the hard places, problems, and power that surround you.

Perspective Changers

Let it marinate and soak in. Repeat three times:

**I have told you this
so that you may have peace.**[68]

The Compiling Game Knockout

Really? It's understandable that you got me the first time, but the fourth and four hundredth time? One of Satan's biggest and best tricks throughout all of history is the compiling game. With this tactic, he often knocks us out of the game before we even get started.

When Satan gets us to focus on our problems instead of God, he wins. He can compile so many good opportunities into our lives that they become problems. They start to overwhelm and crush us. He can also compile so many bad thoughts into our heads that we quit before we even start. When Satan gets us focused on our problems instead of our Provider, he knows he can crush us with the loaded responsibility of fixing or managing what only God was meant to fix.

The most tangible example we see of this in the Bible is Job. What Satan does to Job's real life, he does to our inner self all the time. Job takes blow after blow after big blow all at once.

A servant comes to Job and says, "Job, you lost all your oxen,"

and while he was still speaking another came and said, "you lost all your sheep,"

and while he was still speaking another came and said, "you lost all your camels,"

and while he was still speaking another came and said, "you lost all your your servants,"

and while he was still speaking another came and said, "you lost all yours sons and daughters."

What? How would Job even begin to process this? I know I would probably be thinking, "Whoa, too much to take in. All my wealth, all my life systems, and all my family are thrown out the window in a matter of seconds?"

If that wasn't bad enough, Satan tries to hit him with the "of course that would happen to me right now" moment in his next day. After all this has gone wrong, not only does Satan make Job uncomfortably and miserably sick with irritable scratching, but he even got to Job's last lines of support. You know it's bad when even his own wife and best friends are misunderstanding and giving him bad advice. Of course this would happen…

Satan does this in our lives, but even more regularly, he does this in our heads. He brings up one thing that's undone, and then another, and then another until we are overwhelmed. Or he brings up one argument, and then another, and then another until we are overly mad at that person. Or he brings up one God-given opportunity, and then another, and then another, until he steals all our excitement and we don't even want to touch it anymore. Don't let him win this stunt.

One of the greatest analogies I've ever heard is that love is like manure. When you hoard and pile it up, it rots and smells, but when you spread it out it makes things grow. Satan does this when he turns our opportunities into a pile of problems. He piles the good and bad up, until we just want to faint from it being so overwhelming.

When we take on all of the good or bad in our lives, without sharing it with God and others, we will be crushed. Satan has stolen too much joy from me, retracting back inside of my head under the stress of focusing on time crunches and problems, instead of God's victory, goodness, family, and protection all around me.

Satan's biggest role in my opinion is accuser. And as long as Satan is active in the world accusing and confusing others, this world will always have problems. Even as God's children, he will accuse us as unworthy and unfaithful. If Satan can get us to believe that the unavoidable temptation, faith risks, redemption fighting, and serving opportunities are the same as sin, fun risks, sin punishment, and our earthly curse problems, he can make us feel confused and worthless. And we will live in an eternity of discouragement if we allow the troubles of this incomplete world and our incomplete selves to consume our minds.

That is why we must seek to find the all-consuming God, not only in parts but in every part of our lives. This is why we must trust that He who began the good work forming in us will carry it to completion.[69]

God is a God That Revitalizes

God speaks *life* into us. By now, you have experienced words from people that just kill. They've weighed you down, overwhelmed, and just cut to the core. I used to take it all in as something I just had to accept. I didn't realize that I could reject the false lies that try to enter my head! The Bible says, "Godly sorrow brings life but worldly sorrow brings death" (2 Corinthians 7:10, my paraphrase). Godly sorrow brings *life*. My textbook smarts knew it, but I never connected the accuser to the death list of failures and undone projects that scrolled through my head constantly and overwhelmed me to the point of exhaustion. Or I had at least never distinguished that, if those thoughts aren't life giving, maybe they're not from God, or even myself.

I forgot that the accuser and deceiver had the ability to plant tempting beliefs into my head and, "…a deceitful tongue crushes the spirit" (Proverbs 15:4). How long had I listened to that list in my head that just screamed, *failure!* Over and over again. The phrase in 2 Corinthians 7:10 actually says that, "Godly sorrow brings repentance that leads to salvation and leaves no regret." First off, my unfinished work projects weren't a direct sin issue that always needed my repentance. That was not God. Second, me dwelling on these thoughts was in no way bringing no regret. In actuality, it was bringing me closer to deathblows instead of closer to God or a life-giving attitude that would help me change. If anything, dwelling in those thoughts was adding regrets instead of helping create a God-honoring life.

It wasn't God. It was the evil one spitting out accusations! God challenges, but he doesn't condemn or accuse believers. In a time of questions and unknowns, don't let the devil compound problems in your head. As a believer you are not a failure because of Christ! You simply aren't. You are a child of God.

God's correction and discipline can surely be harsh, but God is life giving, He's a redeemer. "The fear of the Lord is a fountain of life…" (Proverbs 14:27). "A heart at peace gives life to the body…" (Proverbs 14:30). "The tongue that brings healing is a tree of life" (Proverbs 15:4). So any time you are hearing words of death and accusation, make sure to push it back because if they are not life giving, they are definitely not of God.

Focus On the Horizon

It was a horrific stormy day on the water with sea-sick marines leaning and throwing up over the side of the ship as the captain walked up. He told the men to move up to the front of the ship and focus on the steady horizon ahead, instead of the unsteady waves below. After following the captain's suggestion, the men slowly regained control of their rumbling bodies as they focused on the constant in the midst of chaos. In the middle of life's storms, God often echoes the same suggestion to us, "Fix your gaze ahead."[70]

When you learn to drive a car, you find out quickly that you have to look ahead instead of directly down at the road lines to avoid and predict accidents. Good perspective can see the immediate road while focusing beyond to continue moving forward safely. We must fix our eyes on the prize because there will be rough patches. There will be moments we must know how to look beyond our immediate problems.

Those Foggy Days

There will be those cloudy days where it's hard to believe the sun is above the clouds, and it's so foggy that it's impossible to focus on the horizon or see what's directly ahead. You cannot even see far enough in front of you to feel safe while driving a car. Those are the days we must slow down, continue moving forward, and focus on the clear boundary lines God has marked out in his Bible, until we make it safely through by staying in the right lanes and staying extra alert.

In the unknown hard times, we must focus on keeping our character and faith in God. We must move forward with caution while we wait for God to remove the storm, or clear the road. Don't compromise your character and purity in this time. It's funny. Sometimes, God being a lamp to our feet and light to our lives can resemble a blazing sun on a crystal clear day with miles of visibility. Other moments it resembles a car's headlights in the middle of a thick fog or snowstorm with barely enough visibility to slowly move forward. His light is still there but it functions in different ways depending on the season.

Satan's God vs. God's Goal

As mentioned earlier, Satan is trying so hard to get you to quit on life, when God wants you to keep going. Satan wants to focus you on your mistakes and messes. God wants to turn those mistakes into a message. Don't just keep going, keep going to God.

Perspective Changers

Let it marinate and soak in. Repeat three times:

Your word is a light on my path.[71]

Own It

Own Your Preparation Season

You're the problem. Own it. You must own this as a season of preparation, instead of accomplishment. Otherwise your unmet expectations and drive will force you to cheat or quit as the alternative to get your wants. This goes not only for the twenty-one to thirty-year old season of preparation, but for the rest of your life as you work towards becoming a person of heavenly perspective and purpose. Cheating yourself and God by compromising your morals and quitting will never be good preparation.

Own Your Character Choice

If there is something in your life that is bringing you down rather than up, stop it. It's not that easy, but it is. If nothing changes, nothing changes. If you continue to compromise your faith by lying at work, you are not preparing. If you believe it's wrong to have sex with someone before marriage, but you continually are, that's not preparing. If you say everyone is supposed to help those in need, but you are not giving to the poor even when you are poor, that's not preparing. If you know God tells you to rest weekly but you are not giving yourself the opportunity, that's not preparing. Own your beliefs. If you are telling others something, or doing something other than what you know to be true, stop and address it because who you are becoming is more important than where you end up going here on earth. A cheap substitute for focusing on the grace in your life is your pace of life. I would rather start with a few beliefs that I own and grow from starting there, rather than start with twenty opinions that I never truly owned at all. Stop enough to start owning your character choices in this preparation season.

Stop Enough to Change Your Life

Trying harder is not enough. Many people lie to themselves by hearing the Word of God and telling themselves they are going to try harder, but they never truly stop their lives enough to make sure that they are putting into practice what they heard. They hear the Words of God at church and in their heads as they tell themselves they will do better. Yet, they never make it a high enough priority to cause the rest of their lives to stop if unchanged. Their character is less important than their goal. Own it. Either stop to give time to what matters the most, or own that you're living as the world does. At least be adult enough to own that.

Perspective Changers

Let it marinate and soak in. Repeat three times:

Do not merely listen to the word, and so deceive yourselves. Do what it says.[72]

The Promised Unknown

"Can I at least know that I'll get there?" is the real question.

Will you get to enjoy the benefits of an earthly Promised Land? It's not yours to be decided. It is not yours to demand. It's less about getting where you want to go than who God wants you to become. Heaven and God's goodness are a guarantee, but your earthly Promised Land wants are not.

Will you be a Joshua and Caleb who get to enter the earthly Promised Land, or a faithful Moses who died only seeing it from afar? Both end destinations were walked by godly men, but with two totally different life outcomes. Will you get to be a godly hero of faith that conquers kingdoms and lives a long healthy life? Or will you be the godly hero who is beheaded before your *prime* and never sees old age, your great grandchildren, or your earned retirement days?[73] Will you get the privilege of building the dreams God has in store like Solomon's Temple or just envision it from afar like his father David?[74] Like Peter and John, will your life's path be painted and characterized by others as a disciple rebuked by God or loved by God? That is not yours to be decided.[75] And neither reveals whether you were the faithful or a failure.

Whether you get to your earthly Promised Land wants or not, is not a trustworthy indicator to determine whether you are on the right path.[76] Arriving at a temporary goal should not be your rite of passage, because becoming more loving by chasing, changing, and growing closer to God is the greatest purpose and gift we have for being alive today. He will change your perspective, purpose, and person to find peace whether you enter the land here on earth or not.

You're responsible for going to God instead of quitting. For focusing past the hard you are going through, to what you are becoming. You must let God turn your obstacles into opportunities, your setbacks into setups, your mess into a message, your mistakes into a miracle. In the unquestionably hard times of stuck frustrations, don't let these be your healthy determiner of whether your life is faithful or a failure. Form a life habit now of not trying to figure this out alone, but with others. A trusting perspective in God's protection and providing is the only chance you have at experiencing an earthly placement in the Promised Land... and even that is never guaranteed.

Perspective Changers

Let it marinate and soak in. Repeat three times:

"Lord, what about him?"

Jesus answered, "What is that to you? You must follow me." [77]

To the Point

I feel alone in the unknown a lot living in my twenty somethings. Life is a mixed blessing and curse because I don't always know what to do, and it's hard. I have amazing experiences, but I have moments where I still struggle with the overall picture of me feeling in the life rut heading to nowhere with no advice or clue of how to get out.

In our eagerness and desperation, we can completely miss that the major work is still not what is done *through us* at this stage, but what is done *in and to* us in this stage. It is more about who you are *becoming* through your circumstances instead of *getting to* a different circumstance. Too often, I'm looking and striving for what I want to get and accomplish, while overlooking and ignoring who I'm becoming in the process. It will take multiple times, if not hundreds of times for this to sink in.

Sadly, since I can't always help you avoid or alleviate hard, my focus is for you to not just get through it, but to *grow* through it. I want you to end up in God's total love instead of our totally skewed wants. And even though I can't help you avoid hard and I can't tell you what good is to come, I *can* promise that good is coming your way as you continue to follow God. I'm confident of this: you will see the goodness of the Lord here on earth.[78]

So, the goal is to find ourselves as a man or woman of God through His love rites of passage, instead of our careers or family (which are amazing gifts but only cheap substitutes when God comes second). God's secret answer won't answer all of your current wants, but it will give you all the direction you need. Wait for the Lord; be strong and take heart and wait for the Lord."[79] Stop enough to make sure you love yourself, love others, and love God deeper, and God will make the grass greener through you wherever you are planted or passing through.

Perspective Changers

Let it marinate and soak in. Repeat three times:

**I have told you this
so that you may have peace.
In this world you will have troubles,
but take heart,
I have overcome the world.[80]**

Epilogue:
A Young Adult's Charge

Below is my friend's message, which I hope is received as a summarizing encouragement in this transitioning twenty somethings season.

"Don't be afraid of change; embrace it. Welcome it. Throw yourself into it. Precisely because, it is from doing these things that we grow, learn, and mature. You are at a very interesting and exciting point in your life; on the brink of adulthood with adult-like responsibilities and stress, but still possessing the energy and enthusiasm of a young mind, who has yet to truly experience the high highs and low lows that life, in all of it's fullness, has to offer. I don't believe in a superficial God; I believe that a lot of *modern* theology paints God in a fairly unrealistic light. God is not a genie, there to grant us our every wish. I do though, believe in a God that calls us to live near the outermost edges of our comfort zones and calls us, at times, to leap (what some theologians call a *leap of faith*) in to particular unknown abysses. What that abyss may be, exactly, can change from time to time. But most of what it is, is an unknown future; into the very heart of uncertainty. But that's okay. Because we know, that even in the most dark abyss, during the free-fall

of life, we believe in a God who has experienced death and darkness–that was followed
by resurrection and life, and it's this God
that will guide you through the unknown.
It's imperative that through this life, you do all
you can to keep a proper perspective of who you
are. Be true to yourself. Relationships come and
they go. Sometimes the hardest thing to do is
let go. And sometimes the hardest thing to do,
is to be open to the unknown; the future. But
after all, isn't that what life is all about? Being
open to the future? This is exciting stuff! No
matter what, you have to keep reminding yourself, "I will be fine." [81]

Lord, send this out with your pre-grace to prepare and ready hearts to be changed by your perfection in everything.

Endnotes

1   Exodus 38:26; Numbers 1:18-22; Numbers 14:29, 32:11.

2   Exodus 16:2, Exodus 32.

3   Study the Book of Job.

4   Matthew 8:25-26.

5   Luke 5:5.

6   Mark 9:28-29.

7   John 14:5.

8   Matthew 16:9-12.

9   Matthew 8:25-26; John 11:16.

10 Mark 9:32.

11 Matthew 10:16.

12 Mark 8:22-25; Mark 9:25-28.

13 Matthew 19:22; John 6:66.

14 John 16:7 ESV.

15 Romans 8:29.

16 Psalm 23:1.

17 Henri Nouwen, "Moving From Solitude to Community to Ministry," *Leadership* 16 (Springs 1995): 81-87.

18 John 16:33.

19 Roxanne Wieman, "Mark Driscoll Says Just Grow Up," *Relevant Magazine* (Sept 9, 2010).

20 Genesis 41:46. Saul was also made king at thirty (1 Samuel 13:1)!

21 Ecclesiastes 11:9.

22 Exodus 13:17-18.

23 Job 12:24.

24 John 15:19.

25 Francis Chan, *Forgotten God* (Colorado Springs: David C. Cook , 2009), 120.

26 David Klinghoffer, "Saab story–young people in their twenties who think they reflect the values and standards of all people in their twenties through the writings of journalists in their twenties–Column," National Review, March 15, 1993, Findarticles.com, (Aug. 15, 2008).

27 Romans 14:7.

28 John 16:32.

29 Karl Barth quote from Francis Chan's *Forgotten God: Reversing Our Tragic Neglect of the Holy*

Spirit, (Colorado Springs, CO: David C. Cook, 2009), 103.

30 Lamentations 3:55, 57.

31 In 2008 younger baby boomers held an average of 10.5 jobs from ages 18 to 40. *That is an Average of 10.5 Jobs in 22 Years.*

32 Charlie E. "T" Jones.

33 Robert Morgan, *The Read Sea Rules: The Same God Who Led You In Will Lead You Out*, (Nashville, TN: Thomas Nelson, 2001), 6.

34 Cathy Sosoli.

35 My own paraphrase of Hebrews 11:13-15 and 1 Peter 2:11 NLT.

36 Isaiah 50:4; Romans 14:7-8.

37 Psalm 20:4 ESV.

38 Jeremiah 29:11; Rom 8:28; Psalm 37:4.

39 James 4:13-14.

40 Jean Watson, A Caring Moment, Anti Essays, 8 March 2012, http://www.antiessays.com/free-essays/108086.html.

41 Henry Ward Beecher.

42 John Maxwell, *Today Matters: 12 Daily Practices To Guarantee Tomorrow's Success,* (New York, NY: Warner Faith, 2004), 292.

43 Meg Akehi.

44 Psalm 3:5.

45 Ecclesiastes 1:18.

46 Exodus 20:12; Ephesians 6:2; All over Proverbs.

47 Edmund Burke.

48 Galatians 1:10.

49 James Strong, *New Strong's Exhaustive Concordance of the Bible*, (Nashville, TN: Thomas-Nelson Publishers; 1996), *Greek #3809*.

50 Isaiah 30:15-16, 18.

51 Robert Clinton, *The Making Of A Leader,* (Colorado Springs, CO: NavPress, 1988), 35.

52 John Maxwell, *The Five Levels of Leadership*, (New York, NY: Center Street: 2011), 124.

53 Isaiah 29:6, Isaiah 30:30, Jeremiah 23:19, Psalm 29.

54 C.S. Lewis, *The Lion, the Witch and the Wardrobe*, (New York City: HarperCollins, 1950), 146.

55   Jon Acuff, "The god you least expect", January 2012, http://www.jonacuff.com/stuffchristians like/2012/01/the-god-you-least-expect/.

56   Hebrews 11:19.

57   Proverbs 20:24.

58   Jeremiah 29:13.

59   Mark 10:28-29.

60   Meg Akehi.

61   James Strong, *New Strong's Exhaustive Concordance of the Bible*, (Nashville, TN: Thomas -Nelson Publishers; 1996), *Greek #639.*

62   Bill Hybels, *Axiom: Powerful Leadership Proverbs*, (Grand Rapids, MI: Zondervan, 2008), 61.

63   John 12:16.

64   Proverbs 3:5.

65   Romans 12:1-2.

66   Psalms 33:10-11; Acts 5:38-39; Proverbs 19:21.

67   Proverbs 11:7; Proverbs 28:12, 28; Proverbs 29:2.

68   John 16:33.

69   Philippians 1:6.

70 Proverbs 4:25; Hebrews 12:2.

71 Psalm 119:105.

72 James 1:22.

73 Hebrews 11:32-38.

74 1 Chronicles 22:5-10.

75 John 21:22.

76 Psalm 73; Job 21.

77 John 21:21-22.

78 Psalm 27:13; Romans 8:28.

79 Psalm 27:14.

80 John 16:33.

81 Bryan Garner.